Perfume of Silence

Francis Lucille

Compiled by Rupert Spira

Truespeech Productions
P.O.Box 1509
Temecula, CA 92593

www.francislucille.com

First Edition
Printed in the United States of America

ISBN-10: 1882874013

ISBN-13: 9781882874019

1. Spirituality, 2. Consciousness

Other books by Francis Lucille:
     Truth Love Beauty
     Eternity Now

This book is dedicated to all the beautiful beings who have made this publication possible through their labor of love.

Francis Lucille
Temecula, California
2006

Contents

Foreword

Before the formulation of a question there is the feeling, "I don't know." It is out of this openness at the level of the mind that a question comes. This openness is expressed the only way the mind can express something, through concepts, but the true essence of the question is the openness from which it originates. We could say that a question is this openness in the form of a concept; it is the shape that "I don't know" takes in the mind.

When this question is received by someone who is simply present as this openness, the openness again takes the form of conceptual thinking and delivers an answer. The purpose of the answer is not to perpetuate the conceptual thinking that is present in the question, although sometimes a dialogue may take place at that level. The purpose of the answer is to put an end to the question, for a question only ceases to be a question when it is truly answered.

That which puts an end to the question is that which dissolves the concept, the form in which the question was asked, and that into which the question is dissolved is that from which it came in the first place, openness. There is nowhere else for it to go. So we could say that the answer undresses the question and returns us to naked openness, to the original not-knowing.

The difference between the openness before the question and the openness after the answer is simply that, because the question has been satisfactorily answered, there is at least temporarily a cessation of agitation in this openness, there is no impulse to escape from it into conceptual thinking, and in this moment we therefore have a glimpse of our true nature; openness experiences itself as such.

So nothing new is given by the teacher. The question contains the answer, in fact it arises out of the true answer. If this were not the case, if we did not already know the answer, how would we recognize it when we hear it? From where would that "Yes" that we feel when we understand something come from?

The openness from which the question arises and the openness from which the answer comes are not two different opennesses, they are one and the same. The asking of the question is the creative aspect of this openness. Its dissolution is the meditative aspect, the dissolving of all that exists in that which is. If we ask, "What is the purpose of a question? Why this movement, this creativity, why not just rest?" we cannot answer because the mind is itself part of the creativity about which we are asking.

However, William Blake said, "Eternity is in love with the productions of time" and so perhaps it is just that this openness enjoys revealing itself to itself from moment to moment and this play of dialogues is just one of its many modes of enjoyment. It is a game of hide and seek in which it hides itself and reveals itself at its own pleasure.

So the real question is not in the words and the real answer is not in the words either. The words must vanish for their true meaning to be understood and in that moment we realize that we do not understand what is said in these pages; we are that understanding. So the true content of both the answer and the question is this openness, this not-knowing, out of which they both arise, in which they are both maintained, and into which they are both dissolved. It is that which is present behind, between, and within the words.

This book is taken from dialogues with Francis Lucille in America, Canada, and Europe, between 1997 and 2002, but these meetings were not about asking questions and receiving answers and nor is this book. It has nothing to do with the exchange of concepts or with agreeing or disagreeing. If we find ourselves comparing, judging, and analyzing, we have missed the point, we have not yet been undressed. Rather it is a movement from openness to openness. This is the relationship between the student and the teacher. It is a dance that goes nowhere. We formulate questions out of this openness and they are dissolved again into this openness. It is a divine play in which openness reveals itself to itself moment by moment. The steps of this dance are sometimes fast and sometimes slow, sometimes gentle and sometimes austere, sometimes complex and sometimes simple, sometimes intellectual and sometimes heartfelt, sometimes long and sometimes short, but it is always the same dance.

The purpose of these dialogues is love. It is not to reinforce the idea that we are students and that the teacher is a teacher. When this openness is revealed to itself through this play of dialogues, one of the ways it is experienced is as friendship, as love, and this love is the dissolution of boundaries, the dissolution of all the makes us think and feel we are separate from each other and from the world. Strangely enough it is this very dissolution of "other" that makes us truly capable of loving an "other."

Francis Lucille often says that we should forget everything that he says the moment we hear it or read it. What remains is the real meaning of the words, that to which we refer when we say "I," the true answer to the question, the perfume of silence.

R.S.

1

Be Present Without Intention

Why are some experiences, such as a sensation in the body, conceptualized as "me" and others, such as a perception of the world, conceptualized as "not me"?

It is simply because you choose to call some "me" and some "not me." You make an artificial distinction as a result of a conditioned habit. If you had been born in a civilization in which the rising sun was called "my sun," you would consider it your sun. Both the perception that you call "the rising sun" and the sensation that you call "my body" appear in you. Neither is more or less "you" than the other.

The connection I have with my body is different from the connection I have with other bodies. That is why I feel that this body is myself and others are not. For example, I cannot feel the sensations in someone else's body.

I am not denying that you appear to have a special connection with your body. Compare this with your car. When you are driving your car, you see it from the inside, whereas you see all others from the outside. So although you seem to have a special relationship with your car, it doesn't imply that you are your car. It is the same in relation to your body. You are the consciousness in which your body-

5

mind and all other body-minds appear. However, this doesn't imply that you, as consciousness, are only this single body-mind organism or that you are a by-product of it.

The belief that you are in your body is simply an interpretation of your actual experience. It is also an interpretation to think that you have a closer connection with some sensations than with others or to think that some sensations are on the inside and others are on the outside. All you need to do is to see it for what it is: an interpretation.

Such an interpretation may be convenient in some situations, and when it is, we use it. However, beware of becoming attached to an interpretation, of becoming hypnotized by it, and thinking that it is a representation of how things really are.

I am perfectly capable of using the same interpretation as you do when needed, but why not also use the absence of interpretation when it is not required by the circumstances. If in doubt, don't interpret. What something appears to be is not necessarily what it is. What we call "my body" is an interpretation. When we identify with this interpretation, we feel separate, but in the absence of any interpretation, we discover that our body is consciousness.

Our real body includes the mind and the entire universe. This is the body we have always had and the one in which all bodies, gross and subtle, come into existence. We are not interested in what things appear to be, but in what things really are. It is important to be aware of what is fact and what is interpretation. Never take interpretation for fact.

We never actually experience the body as we conceive of it. We experience sensations, and it is only a subsequent interpretation that tells us, "This sensation arose in my foot." At the time of the sensation, our foot was not present and our body was not present, only the sensation was present.

It is dangerous to use a theory as a tool in a domain for which it is not suited. For instance, the materialist interpretation of our experience, which is suitable for use in relation to the physical world, is not efficient in relation to happiness, love, or beauty, because it is not the appropriate tool.

6

How do we decide which tool to use?

Use the one that works. This materialist interpretation of the nature of reality is the most prevalent interpretation of the world in which we live and it is obviously a failure in terms of happiness. The most secure basis is one in which there is no interpretation. Then, depending on the circumstances, we use whatever theory is appropriate, knowing that all theories are limited, all are provisional. If they can do the job, we use them. If they can't, we place them back in the toolbox where they belong.

Although consciousness is the screen on which everything appears, that which happens on the screen is different for each of us, and we identify with our own picture.

We can only use metaphors up to a point. When stretched too far they don't work. We use the metaphor of images on a television screen to understand the relationship of thoughts, feelings, and perceptions to consciousness. The screen stands for consciousness, and the images for the manifestations, the energies, the appearances.

If we want to understand the relationship between consciousness and the apparent multiplicity of minds, we can also use the image of a television screen, but in a different way. If innumerable television screens, each with their own image, represent innumerable minds, then in this case, consciousness is indicated by an observer who is watching all the television screens at the same time. Sometimes two images may have some connection because they share a common object. Sometimes they may not seem to have any connection, because their fields don't intersect. However, one single witness observes all screens. In this metaphor the witness stands for consciousness and each screen stands for each individual mind.

This individual consciousness does not seem to share in the totality.

Objectively it is limited, but subjectively it is not. One television screen cannot see the other screens, but the observer has access to all of them. In the same way, your mind does not have access to other minds, but one consciousness sees all minds. The observer is not foreign to you because it is you. It is seeing and understanding these words right now. There is not a separate consciousness for each mind. There is only one hearer, one seer, one perceiver. The apparatus with which we see is by itself inert, unable to see. A telescope is useless without an astronomer behind it. It doesn't see anything by itself. Likewise, the apparatus of mind doesn't see anything by itself.

So the place to reside is in the witnessing consciousness?

It is not even a place to reside. It is the place where we always naturally reside, so no effort is needed to reside there. We simply have to understand this. It may seem difficult to reside there, but it is impossible not to reside there.

One is occasionally jerked out of it and then periodically one gets back there.

We occasionally seem to be jerked out of consciousness, but in fact, we never are. For instance, as long as we feel that it is a problem to be jerked out of consciousness, this feeling itself seems to jerk us out. The moment we understand that whatever happens, we are the consciousness in which it is happening, then being apparently jerked out of it is no longer a problem. In just the same way, falling asleep is not a problem because we know that the dream we are going to have is an illusion.

I feel as if I am looking out of this body and not out of that table. So, although that which sees is obviously infinite, it appears to have a limited or individual view.

That understanding is the core of what could be called en-lightenment. We have to move away from the limitations that are superimposed onto consciousness. We have to dissociate con-sciousness, which is subjective and universal, from mind, which is objective and personal.

Somehow they reside hand in glove.

They are hand in glove in the sense that an object cannot appear without consciousness. However, the mind is an object that comes and goes. Everything that is objective is limited. The subject has no limitations. We superimpose the limitations of the object onto the subject that is unlimited. It is unlimited because it is not objective and therefore has no shape. If it has no shape, it has no contour, no borders. If it had borders we would be able to perceive them. If we could see the borders, the limits of consciousness, there would have to be a different consciousness that perceived them.

The truth is that although it seems to you that consciousness is limited, it is not actually your experience. It seems to you that way, but it is a trick. This trick is called Maya. We seem to have the experience of a limited consciousness but when we investigate more closely, we see that it is impossible. That which is aware of limitations transcends limitations and is therefore beyond them.

What is the function of the mind in this process?

First, we eliminate all beliefs about consciousness. These beliefs are very subtle. We depersonalize consciousness. For that part of the journey the mind can be used because it is the mind that has personalized consciousness in the first place. That which has done the thing has to undo it. However, the mind cannot go further than that and, at this point, we understand clearly that a personal consciousness is not our experience. This is very important. Although it seems to be our experience that consciousness is personal, in fact it is not. That is as far as we can go with the mind. At this point, we are open to the dimension of consciousness that lies beyond the mind.

The mind then becomes silent. This is not an artificial silence but a natural silence, when the mind has reached its limits and cleansed itself of all accumulated theories. Then for a while the question is dropped and in the absence of any question, the sense of separation vanishes. We now find ourselves in a welcoming presence in which the stage has been prepared for the permanent miracle, for

9

beauty, love, and fulfillment. We are open to it. When we have reached the outposts of the mind, we are ready for the journey to the heart.

Is it possible to move into the heart before reaching the frontiers of the mind?
Absolutely.

♋

If I ask myself, "Who am I?" I often get a feeling in the heart area. Is this a limitation that ties one to the body?

If you ask the question, "Who am I?" and look for the answer, it seems to come from this area. However, this area is a perceived object. It is a perception or a sensation. The real "you" is the consciousness to which this heart object appears. Do not rest on any object thinking, "This is me." This is the meaning of the saying, "The Son of Man has no place to rest his head." You cannot find yourself as an object, whether this object is profane, sacred, gross, or subtle. Don't allow yourself to rest on any object.

Would you say that the highest point in meditation would be to rest in the heart?

It is certainly not to meditate upon any object and certainly not to meditate in the heart. Meditation is to simply let your thoughts, feelings, and perceptions freely evolve without any agenda. Remember when, as a very young baby, you had just been changed and fed and were not tired enough to sleep. What does a baby do in such a situation? It is simply present without any intention. That's meditation.

10

Meditation is not an effort. The posture is important but only insofar as it allows the body to be as transparent, as inconspicuous as possible. It is important to avoid a big pain in the middle of the picture. The correct position for meditation is the one that serves this purpose. Don't forget that we are on the direct path. Why postpone happiness? To create pain in the present in order to secure hypothetical happiness in the future is not consistent with the direct path.

Meditation is very simple. It means to surrender the mind, the body, and the world, from moment to moment, to the silent presence in which they appear. That's all.

What does it mean to surrender the mind, the body, and the world to that in which they appear? How do we do that?

Surrender the one who does that. Surrender the one who does anything, who wants anything, who is afraid of anything. This one is an appearance. This one is made of thoughts and feelings. When this one is silent, then the world, the body, and the mind are surrendered to silence.

Nothing else needs to be done. It is only if it seems to you that you are not in the enlightened state and that something needs to be done, that you have apparently lost the enlightened state. You are in the enlightened state all the time. The only moment when you are apparently not in the enlightened state is when the doer, the desirer, pops up. It appears either as a thought or a feeling in the body, a resistance, an "I-don't-want-this-feeling" or "that's-not-the-way-things-should-be."

The biggest obstacle on the path is to think that the natural state is necessarily a pleasurable one. In such a case, every state that is deemed non-pleasurable is immediately rejected and we appear to fall from our enlightened state. To surrender the world means that nothing pleasurable attracts us and we feel no repulsion for anything that is unpleasant.

That is easy under peaceful circumstances. At such times, grace makes everything easy. Nothing attracts us or distracts us. The world is surrendered. The song of the birds, the traffic noises, the

11

fragrance and the temperature of the air we are breathing, whatever we are experiencing in the moment, all come and go freely, without triggering the slightest reaction, without making waves. That teaches us what the enlightened state is like.

All we have to do is to transpose what is true of the world in such a situation, to the realm of thoughts and bodily sensations. We welcome our thoughts and bodily sensations in exactly the same way as we welcome the song of the birds, the traffic noise, or whatever it is we are experiencing. When the song of the birds, or whatever it is we are experiencing, is present, it is simply present. We have no agenda with it. We don't do anything to make it appear, to make it stay, or to make it disappear.

The same thing is true of our thoughts and bodily sensations. There is no attachment. Don't stick to anything. The song of the birds, the sound of the traffic, our thoughts and feelings, are dreamlike events. In a way, they are non-events because they don't trigger any activity in us. Of course, if a response is required, then we respond appropriately from this uninvolved perspective, but no trace is left after the response, which could then be a trigger for further thoughts or feelings. We return to openness, ready for the next appearance, whatever it may be.

How can we transpose this welcoming of sounds in the world to the realm of thoughts and bodily sensations?

Go back to your actual perception of the song of the birds or the sound of the traffic. See what is going on. All these perceptions are free-floating in space. Ask yourself, "Where do they appear?" If the answer is that the bird is singing 50 feet from here, see that this is not actually your experience, that it is a concept. The actual experience of the sound is happening at a zero distance from you, not 50 feet away. It is not happening there but rather here, always. Everything is always happening here and now.

The space in which the bird sings is not a geometric or a physical space. It is a different kind of space, which we could call the "here-and-now space." Everything that is occurring, is occurring in this space. We could call it consciousness. It is empty, in the sense that we cannot grasp it with the mind. It has no texture, color, shape, or solidity. However, this does not imply that it is not present. Presence is its quality. It is consciousness, awareness, clarity, transparency.

All thoughts, feelings, and perceptions are free-floating in this space. The song of the birds or the sound of the traffic point towards it. Once recognized, this space becomes very easy to experience. The body (that is, sensations and feelings) and the mind (that is, thoughts and images) are also appearances that arise in this same "here-and-now space." In fact, there is no separation between the world, the mind, and the body. They are all appearances within this space. See that this space is limitless, because any boundary is simply another perception or appearance within it. The boundary is limited both in space and time, because it has a beginning and an end. This space is unlimited and therefore timeless.

Now is the key to welcoming the body and the mind. This "here-and-now space" is the key. It is the bridge that enables us to transpose the enlightened state with respect to the world, to an enlightened state with respect to the body and the mind. Let thoughts, feelings, and bodily sensations unfold freely in this space, just as you let perceptions, such as the song of the birds and the sound of my voice, freely unfold. Know that they are not separate. This is the experience of our true nature in the presence of objects.

It is so easy to lose this experience.

If it seems that you are losing it, just go back to the sound of the birds or the traffic, or whatever it is that you are experiencing, and it will guide you. Allow it to reveal the presence in which it appears. Let it flow through you and see that you are that through which it flows.

Don't fall back into thinking or feeling that something should be different, that enlightenment is for tomorrow. Every "now" moment is an opportunity for enlightenment. Every future or past moment is a non-opportunity for enlightenment.

This presence is completely independent of whatever is appearing within it, just as the mirror is not stained, disturbed, or destroyed by the images it reflects. This presence is like a mirror without borders. Everything is reflected within it. Nothing limits it. It seems to be contained within the body-mind, but in fact it contains the whole universe and everything that exists. If it could speak it would say, "I contain everything that exists within myself. I am the true nature of everything that exists and you are that."

The idea that this presence is limited is simply a limited concept appearing within this unlimited presence. The feeling that this presence is limited is simply a limited sensation appearing within this same unlimited presence. Apart from these superimposed belief systems and contractions, this presence is free from limitations. This presence is our common treasure, our true father and our true, divine mother. Offer your mind and your body to this presence.

When I meditate I do not experience the feeling that this is pure consciousness.

That is because you are expecting something to happen. This expectation is an escape from what is. It is an escape from the current situation, from your own fear, from your own sense of lack, from whatever you are feeling. See why you feel that things are not the way they should be. Where does the feeling that something needs to be done, fixed, or perfected, come from? Whenever you feel that things are not as they should be, take a look at the origin of this feeling, instead of becoming its slave and starting the big search for enlightenment. Just see this feeling for what it is. When the sense of lack no longer arises, then you are fulfilled. Fulfillment is the absence of lack. Just enjoy yourself. Be like the baby.

Sometimes there is nothing, no enjoyment, and the emotions are quiet.

When you say there is no enjoyment it means that, in your opinion, things are not as they should be. What makes you feel that there is no enjoyment? It is a label that we put on a situation when we feel there is a lack. Explore the lack when it arises; welcome it. Do not do anything to eliminate it, just be interested in it. Let the lack arise without interfering with it, without blindly doing what it tells you to do.

When I look, the mind seems to block me.

This lack is not just in the mind, it is a feeling also, a sensation in the body. In order to explore this lack, you have to look in the body as well as the mind. If you completely welcome the lack or the boredom, it may evolve and reveal other feelings. Just let it be present in you, don't try to eliminate it. It is not going to kill you. It just consists of sensations in the body.

When I sit on my own without a teacher, I cannot become still.

Where is it you cannot go? Just start where you are, with whatever is present in the moment. Meditation is like washing dishes; we always start with the dish on the top of the pile. If we start with the dish on the bottom, we are in trouble! The top dish is the one that is appearing to you right now. It is whatever you are experiencing right now. So start meditation in the now, not in the future.

When I start in the now I feel a drag into unconsciousness.

This drag is localized in your body; it has a certain texture. At some point, it is accompanied by images in the mind. You have to explore, but don't be bored or afraid of your boredom or fear. Be interested, because your boredom and fear are resisting this exploration.

Up to now, the resistance seems to be more powerful than my ability to deal with it.

Your fear is not going to kill you. Just allow it to be present. It is not a problem. Treat it like a television show. You must be interested in discovering this sense of separation in yourself. It is this same sense of separation that has made you miserable, so it is important to discover it. Don't try to go and get it. If it doesn't appear, just live happily. If it appears and starts making your life miserable, then face it, be interested in it. Do not face it in order to destroy it but rather say, "Show me what you are made of, if you want me to obey you."

What is the difference between being interested in a feeling and asking the question, "Who is having this feeling?"

There is no difference because the feeling of boredom, fear, lack, is the apparent one who is having this feeling. It is the ego. However, in self-inquiry we are not interested in who is having the feeling, but in what is the source of the I-thought, the I-feeling, the ego. It is not about the ego itself. We go upstream from the feeling to the ego and from the ego to its source. When we reach this sense of lack that has no cause, we have already reached the legs and the arms of the ego.

Is it possible to investigate the fundamental nature of consciousness? Whenever I look and see that consciousness is present, there is, at the same time, always the appearance of objects.

If there were only the appearance of objects, we wouldn't have invented the words "I" or "consciousness." The word "consciousness" refers to that which is present during the presence of objects and between their appearances. In order to answer the question as to whether or not we are a conscious being, we must first go to that place from which the certainty of our answer "Yes" comes. The mind ceases to exist when we reach that place. It has no memory of that place in which it is absent. However, that doesn't imply that this consciousness without an object is not experienced.

When we ask ourselves, "Am I a conscious being?" we pause for a moment and then answer with absolute certainty, "Yes." What happens in that pause? The mind cannot say because the experience has no objective qualities that can be remembered or formulated. However, it is from precisely this non-objective experience that our certainty is derived. This certainty is very different from the certainty derived from an object-based experiment. Any object-based experiment could be a mirage. For instance, if we say, "I saw my shirt on the bed," we may have been mistaken. We all know examples of thinking we had seen something, but not having done so. Therefore, object-based knowledge is always under legitimate suspicion, but not consciousness, because we have no doubt that we are conscious. It shines with absolute certainty. It is knowledge of a different order.

In fact it is not appropriate to use the word "knowledge" in this context because, in our normal understanding of the word, "knowledge" always refers to an object. The words "consciousness," "love," "happiness," and "beauty" don't refer to objects. The experience they refer to is timeless and objectless, and therefore doesn't leave any trace in memory, although it transforms the mind. That is what happens when we understand something. In the moment of understanding a sentence for instance, the sentence itself has ended, has ceased to exist. The understanding takes place in a timeless moment when the mind, the content of the sentence, is not present. The mind subsequently reappears with the formulation of the understanding. However, the moment of understanding itself is timeless, it is an experience of our true nature. It is consciousness experiencing itself. After the understanding the mind is transformed, its content is changed. Consciousness has power over the mind, the body, and the world.

What is meant by saying the world does not exist if I am not looking at it?

We have to be careful when we say, "The world does not exist if I am not looking at it." "I" in this case refers to consciousness, so in effect the statement could be reformulated, "The world does not exist if it is not appearing in consciousness." This doesn't imply that the world does not exist if it is not appearing in this specific mind. There is a big difference. For instance, London may not be appearing to you right now, but I am sure that it is appearing to a few people. Therefore, to say that London doesn't exist because it is not appearing to this specific mind, is not what is implied by the statement, "If London is not appearing it does not exist."

Any object is simply its appearance in consciousness. This understanding frees us from the notion of a world existing "out there," separate and independent from consciousness. It doesn't imply that the content of the mind is all that exists. It means that all that exists is in consciousness. To think that everything that exists is in the mind, is a position of madness. It is solipsism. For the one who takes this position, everything seems to make sense, but everybody else can see that he is crazy. What we are talking about here is a totally different kind of solipsism. It is one in which only consciousness is and this consciousness is not personal.

How do we recognize consciousness? It feels as if consciousness recognizes itself.

Yes, but this recognition is not in the mind. The mind is an agency that can formulate this recognition. However, in the absence of a mind, there cannot be any formulation. However, this doesn't imply that the recognition has not taken place.

Consciousness doesn't need any agent to know itself. It knows itself by itself. It shines by itself, just like the sun. It does not need an external consciousness to see it. The moon needs the light of the sun to be seen. In this analogy the moon is like the ego. The ego looks like consciousness, just as the moon has a round shape like the sun and seems to shine like the sun. However, the moon is not autonomous; it does not shine with its own light. It is an object that shines with the reflected light of the sun. In other words the I-thought or I-feeling is not the sun; it is only the moon. It requires consciousness to be seen, to shine.

Consciousness knows itself by itself. We do not need anybody to tell us that we are conscious, we know it. We knew it as a newborn baby even before we knew language. Even before we were born we knew ourselves as a conscious being. We have forgotten that we are this consciousness and have identified ourselves with objects. We think, "I am the body, therefore I am going to die." However, consciousness doesn't find itself in a body. The body appears in consciousness, the mind appears in consciousness, the world appears in consciousness. That is our experience. In spite of this, we superimpose the opposite notion onto our experience, that consciousness is in the mind, that the mind is in the body, and that the body is in the world.

Is it possible for this identification to come to an end?

Yes, of course, because it is an object. The identification is not real. It is only a belief. The moment we understand that the illusion comes and goes, it is no longer a problem, because it is seen for what it is. When we watch a film on television, we know that it is not for real and therefore we are not truly afraid. We enjoy the film knowing that it comes and goes. It is possible to discover this extraordinary way of being in the world without being of the world. We enjoy the film without being a hundred percent absorbed in it. In the absence of this attitude, we suffer.

When intense feelings come, they seem to cover everything else completely, and there always seems to be a battle going on between non-identification and getting drawn back into these intense feelings.

If they really cover everything, there is nothing you can do. Fortunately they are states, so they don't last. First find the truth when you are at peace. Investigation initially requires peaceful conditions. Once we have understood the nature of these feelings, we can go back to the world and put our understanding to the test. It is easy to be happy in our bedroom. It is less easy to be happy on the London Underground, so use the Underground as an exercise. Do whatever makes you happy, but understand that it is never an object, a person, that makes you happy. It is always the divine presence.

C3

Everything I know in life, both within myself and in the outside world, is changing from moment to moment. What, therefore, can be truly relied upon?

We can be certain of two things. The first is that there is consciousness, "I am-ness," that we exist. Whatever this consciousness is, it is that which we refer to as "I."

The second thing we can be sure of is that something exists. When we have any experience, we are sure that there is something rather than nothing. This "something" we call "reality." We may not be sure what the nature of this "something" is; nevertheless, we are sure that there is "something." We can be absolutely certain of these two facts alone.

We are not sure what the true nature of this "I" or this "something" is, but the problem is not our uncertainty. The problem is our pseudo certainties, our beliefs as to what this "I" and this "something" really are. For instance, we believe that "I," consciousness, is contained within the mind, and that this mind is itself contained within the body. However, if we ask ourselves, "How do I know this?" we discover that there is actually no experiential evidence that corroborates this assertion. It is simply a belief that we have adopted. However, if we adopt what is being said here as a new belief, it makes our case even worse: not only do we harbor the original belief, but now another one has been added to it. So we have to find out for ourselves whether it is true or not that consciousness arises in the body or the mind.

If we claim that consciousness arises in the body, there must be something present to witness its arising. Likewise, if we claim that consciousness arises in the mind then, prior to its arising, that is, in the absence of consciousness, there must be something present to experience its arising. If there *is* something present to witness consciousness as it arises, then this something would itself be what we call "consciousness." If there is nothing present to witness the arising of consciousness, then we cannot legitimately make the claim that it arises in the body or the mind. Therefore, either way, when we say or think that consciousness is in the body or in the mind, it is false knowledge. If we take a closer look as to what this false knowledge does for us in our lives, we see that it generates confusion and misery.

If we take the other side of the equation that relates to objects, to things, to our experience and certainty that there is something rather than nothing, whatever this "something" actually is, we have to see clearly that these objects, whatever their ultimate reality, always appear in consciousness. Therefore, our access to their reality, to the true nature of whatever is experienced, is always made through consciousness. This is very important and is usually ignored. We presume that we have direct access to things in themselves and that these things exist independent from consciousness, but it is not so. Whatever we experience, we always experience it through consciousness. However, we have excluded consciousness from our model of reality, which is considered to exist independently of it.

What evidence do we have that reality, the true nature of things, is independent of consciousness? Absolutely none. We believe it to be true without evidence. If we ask ourselves if we have ever experienced anything without consciousness the answer is unequivocally, "No!" However, with the same conviction and in flagrant contradiction to our actual experience, we maintain that objects exist independent and separate from consciousness. This conviction is the root cause of conflict and misery.

However, we should not adopt this new perspective, but simply liberate ourselves from the belief that reality is independent of consciousness. We are then open to another possibility in which reality, the ultimate nature of things, arises out of consciousness and is therefore one with it. After all, that is our actual experience.

The approach to a true understanding of objects, that bypasses the presence of consciousness, is self-limiting, because our knowledge of the reality of objects can only be as good as our knowledge of consciousness. The scientific approach to reality ignores this fact on purpose. It limits its investigation to the realm of the phenomena of the world, forgetting the fact that they are inseparable from consciousness. Therefore, the knowledge that is secured through these means is inherently limited, because the scope of the investigation is limited from the outset.

If the only path to absolute knowledge is through consciousness, how are we going to proceed? Simply by seeing, by looking. Consciousness, that which we are absolutely certain of, whatever it is, is also that which we call "I." However, we have overlooked this "I," we have forgotten our Self, we have excluded it from the way we view and understand the world, and have superimposed onto it beliefs, concepts, and feelings that have been inherited from our surroundings, from our experiences, and perhaps even from our genes.

All that needs to be done to realize the true nature of reality is to liberate consciousness from the accumulated beliefs, concepts, and feelings that we have superimposed upon it. We do this simply through seeing, through welcoming. For this to be accomplished we need a certain quality of energy, of intensity, which I call love for the truth.

2

There Is No "There"

Very little seems to be said about emotions in this approach.

We are not interested here in the story of our lives, in what happened to us when we were young, and so on. The root of all that drama is taken care of by freeing thoughts, sensations, and perceptions from their association with a personal entity. We don't have to follow the story downstream to all the apparent causes in the past, because that would take us nowhere. We just stay with the current story, the present situation, without interpretation or interference, and this takes us naturally upstream to the source. At the end of the story we don't need to tell the story; we simply note the absence of a storyteller.

We have to be careful of any approach in which we feel that we have to get rid of something. Every time that we feel that we get rid of something, we remain as the "feeler" getting rid of something. In this case we get rid of one contraction but create another subtler entity, the one who has eliminated the problem. The one who has eliminated the problem is the continuation of the problem.

The ego thinks that this approach is ineffective because it claims, "I don't see myself dying." However, it is not possible for the ego to be the witness of its own disappearance. This approach doesn't leave any hope or food for the ego, the person, the drama. In this sense, it is very dry. However, when the ego is not present, true emotion, true beauty, true love, and true impersonality blossom. When we are unencumbered by the drama, we have a deep connection with others. We see their beauty and their love for the truth. At the moment we see this love of the truth in someone, we are touched very deeply at a place where we are one.

What do you mean by "going upstream to the source"?

It means going from the uncomfortable feeling, whatever it is, to the source in which it appears and out of which it is ultimately made. First of all, the feeling is divested of its psychological content, the "I" element, around which it revolves and upon which it depends. This is accomplished simply by understanding that this "I" element is in fact non-existent. This understanding is the accomplishing agent. We simply return to this understanding, and the "I" element is naturally dropped as a result. In this way, the uncomfortable feeling is downgraded to the status of a bodily sensation rather than a feeling. It is simply experienced as a sensation appearing in our benevolent, indifferent presence. We have no agenda with the sensation, positive or negative. It is just experienced for what it is, a neutral sensation. Because it is no longer coveted or rejected, the sensation is free to evolve, remain, or vanish in its own time and we are free to remain as we are, the freedom in which it appears, the source.

See that it is your experience that everything is free-floating in awareness, no matter how delightful, painful, or neutral the situation. It is always so. When that is understood, the situation is always neutral and awareness always delightful.

What do you mean by "true emotion?" All my emotions feel real.

"True emotion" refers to any emotion that does not depend on a separate "I" entity for its existence. Negative emotion always has this apparent separate entity for its foundation.

Is it possible to be enlightened without the mind having any knowledge of it?

Yes, because the symptoms of enlightenment are not necessarily apparent to the mind right away. To begin with, the mind may not be aware of enlightenment because there may not be, as yet, any traces of destruction in it. The mind becomes aware of it at a later stage when the signs of destruction are visible everywhere.

At some point, the mind notices that it has become like a child again, happy and free. However, these kinds of signs come later. In the beginning enlightenment is a non-event for the mind. There are instances in which there is a big explosion at some point, a point of no return, but it is not necessarily the case. If you have come here with a sincere desire for the truth, which only you can ascertain in your heart, then either it has already happened or it is imminent. The mind will gradually know, when it sees the destruction of the old patterns of fear and desire.

I don't feel enlightened or even near enlightenment.

The person who does not feel enlightened or near to it, can never be enlightened, unenlightened, near to it, or far from it. This entity does not exist other than the thought or feeling "I." This thought or feeling "I" appears in enlightenment, which is always present, but also has the capacity to temporarily and apparently veil it. This veiling capacity is called Maya.

I have very strong opinions and don't want to give them up.

That's your problem! You'll be screwed up by those who have the same opinions as you and by those who have the opposite opinions. You have to give up everything, not only your opinions, but also your

25

life. See how understanding comes about through intelligence. Understanding is always the result of giving up some past opinions. For instance, Einstein discovered the theory of relativity by giving up the notion of an absolute system of reference in time and space.

It is always through giving up concepts and opinions that we make progress. When we give up all opinions, then we make absolute progress, which means progress towards the Absolute. It doesn't mean that there is no activity, that you accept everything passively. We can simply see the facts in any situation, without strong opinions, take action, and forget whatever has happened.

There is no need to form a philosophy to oppose a belief. The opposite of a system is more or less the same as that which it opposes. For example, communism and capitalism are both related to greed. When you see that what you are opposing is just more of the same thing, you drop it and go your way.

You might think that this approach is not efficient, but honesty is always efficient. It may not seem so straight away, but it has long-term, positive effects. Honesty, truth, and love never die. They remain alive in the hearts of people. They are like a torch. They pass on from generation to generation. Of course, if you see a problem in society and there is something that you can do about it, go ahead and do it.

 හ

What is the experience of consciousness and where is it recognized?

At this moment, you are understanding these words. That "you," which is understanding these words right now, is consciousness. It is very simple. From moment to moment, there is presence. This consciousness is always present, under all conditions and in all circumstances. You cannot turn it on and off. It is always present in the background of all perceptions and activities. It is what we refer to as "I." The problem occurs when we identify this consciousness with a

26

personal entity, a body-mind, which is in fact a perceived object. This object is made of memories at the level of thinking, and habits or patterns of behavior at the level of feeling and acting.

There is nothing wrong with the body or the mind. The only problem is that we identify our witnessing presence, consciousness, with them. As long as we identify this witnessing presence with the body and the mind, there is no room for this presence to reveal itself in all its glory. We could say that it reveals itself through a veil. This veil is made of the I-thought and the I-feeling. When it reveals itself in all its glory, which could be called enlightenment, we realize that it is not personal. It realizes its universal nature. We all have it in common. It is the source of all things. It is beyond time. It is eternal. It is absolute splendor, love, and happiness. However, we have to disentangle consciousness from the body-mind mechanism. That is accomplished by understanding the distinction between the perceived and that which perceives. The body and the mind are perceived. Consciousness is that which perceives all things, all thoughts and feelings.

If I hear your words, doesn't that imply duality?

At the time of hearing there is no hearer and there are no words. There is only hearing. Check this for yourself. Ask yourself, "Can I separate myself, consciousness, from the sound that is present?" No! They are one. So the separation is not actually experienced. The experience of hearing happens here, at a zero distance from myself, from consciousness. However, it is followed by the afterthought, "*I* was the hearer of these words." With this thought the subject, "I," and the object, "words," are created. That is how duality is created. However, this thought is in turn inseparable from consciousness. It is again perceived at a zero distance from consciousness. There is no thinker and no thought, there is only thinking. In the now, in the truth of our experience, there is no distance, no separation. Everything is here; there is no "there." Duality is never actually experienced. That is why it is called the "illusion of ignorance" and not just "ignorance."

27

Many times, when I am alone and ask, "What am I?" there is a deep longing.

This sense of longing is a perception. Are you the perception or the space in which it appears? You are not this longing and it is not always present. It comes and goes. You are not the perception, you are that in which it appears. However, you can never perceive this space in which it appears. If you could it would, by definition, be a perception. Our actual experience is that we are nothing objective.

The next step is to live in accordance with this understanding. If it becomes unclear again and we find ourselves thinking or feeling that we are located somewhere or that we are limited, we have to return to this understanding. We have to be serious and honest, and try to find what we really are, because we don't want to spend our lives serving something that does not exist. If I am the servant of something, then at the least I want to know what it is that I am serving. We should serve that space, that awareness, that presence, which we can never see objectively and which is at the same time undeniable. We know that it is undeniable because if it were not present nothing else could exist.

When you do anything, see whether this activity is undertaken as a servant of this presence or as the slave of a shadow, a personal entity. In the beginning, this may seem theoretical and the mind will come up with resistances such as, "This is theoretical; forget it." This thought, however, is one of the ways the separate entity tries to protect itself. The real question is not whether it is theoretical, but whether or not it is true.

If the answer is, "Yes, my activity is serving a separate entity," then we have to investigate this entity, this "I." This "I" is a perceived object. To what does it appear? It appears in the real "I," consciousness. In this way we move from the object to its source. At this moment, we get a glimpse of our true nature. After some time, because of the habit of always thinking or feeling ourselves as objects, we find that we cannot remain simply as this objectless presence. Again, the feeling of separation returns, with its customary train of thoughts and activities. However, the mind has been struck a mortal blow by this encounter with the unknown, and its capacity to convincingly impersonate the real "I" has been irreparably weakened.

How should we approach the small "I" when it returns?

We simply return to the understanding that it appears in the real "I." The thoughts that relate to the small "I" will gradually subside. Do not replace them with anything. There will now be gaps in our experience that were formerly occupied by the thoughts and feelings of the small "I." Later we recognize these gaps as our original openness.

To begin with these gaps seem to appear, from time to time, between two thoughts or feelings. Later on we discover that it is in fact the thoughts and feelings that appear, from time to time, in the timeless presence of consciousness. So, from the point of view of mind, these gaps appear fleetingly in the stream of thoughts and feelings. However, from the point of view of consciousness, it is the thoughts and feelings that appear fleetingly in the ocean of consciousness.

Why is it so difficult to remain as this open space of consciousness?

It is actually impossible not to remain as this open space of consciousness. However, to be it knowingly is a different matter. The reason is that once the I-thought has disappeared as a result of understanding, new layers of feeling come to the surface. Unlike the thoughts of the small "I," which seem to hold some promise of happiness, of fulfillment, these feelings are uncomfortable and we therefore try to escape from them into thinking. Thus the process of avoidance through thinking and subsequent activity is again generated. It requires great courage, love, and patience to face these feelings without wanting to escape from them.

છ

I know theoretically that I am love, happiness, and joy, and that everything else is unreal, but this is not actually experienced.

You cannot claim that you are love, happiness, and joy, and at the same time claim that this is not experienced. If it is not experienced, go to that place that you call "I" and don't superimpose the notions of love, happiness, and joy onto it. This place is neutral. Truth is neutral, colorless. This presence is neutral, just like a mirror that allows all pleasant and unpleasant images to be reflected within it. Consciousness is transparent. It has no characteristics of its own. It is pure availability. It is the welcoming of all things: your thoughts, the world, and your body—not the concept of the body but the actual experience of it.

It is important not to reject the body without welcoming it. Don't escape from it into thinking. Experience deeply the richness of the body, like the intricacy of an ancient carpet. It is not something you can explore in one moment. Therefore, first discover the truth as this neutral space of openness, of welcoming, and later on, you will discover that it manifests as love, happiness, and joy.

The truth is that which *is*, the facts without any preferences, the facts unfolding in your benevolent presence. Observe the facts as a scientist would observe a new species of bacterium. They have a life of their own. We are the welcoming presence in which they appear. At some point the perfume of this presence will become manifest.

However, for the time being, your body is largely unknown territory. You have to welcome it, explore it, make acquaintance with the richness of this web of subtle contractions, tensions, and dynamics, without naming it, without calling it fear, desire, or boredom. If you want to name it, call it "interesting stuff," but don't meddle with it. The scientist doesn't want to kill the bugs. He wants to see how they live, reproduce, move, and eat. In the same way, we don't want to kill these sensations, these feelings. We want to understand them. We want to see the richness and the diversity of what we call "me," because we usually avoid it. The moment we see our desire to change things, we are free from it.

30

So it is not up to me to feel the joy, but rather to see the separation clearly.

If "seeing it" becomes another activity that we do, it is an obstacle. The doer is not investigating; it is being investigated. "Investigated" means contemplated. Don't focus on the doer. Let go of the doer whenever something else arises in consciousness. Contemplate whatever appears in the now. If the doer appears in the now, welcome it. If it leaves, let it go.

Welcome whatever appears in the now from moment to moment. Allow whatever arises spontaneously in the now to flow through you without trying to grasp it, resist it, or memorize it. That which comes unexpectedly in the now always comes from grace, from silence. That which comes from silence resonates with silence in us. It reveals silence.

I find that seeing something and naming it are almost inseparable.

Don't name your naming. After all, when you are naming, that is what is present in the now. Don't make it a problem. It is just an old habit of grasping with the mind. Don't try to get rid of it. It is enough just to see it. Of course, there are times when naming is necessary, and then we simply use this tool and replace it in the toolbox when it is no longer required.

Thought is not the thing that it refers to. It is a theory. The theory of a thing is not the thing itself. Thought doesn't lead to reality. It only takes us to its own ending.

ℭ

Where does understanding happen?

Understanding doesn't happen in the mind. We may ponder a question and at some point the question vanishes and we have a flash of understanding, of insight. When the question is present, the answer, the understanding, is absent. Likewise, when the answer appears, the question has by definition disappeared. Then we say, "Now I have the answer." However, between asking the question and formulating the answer, the mind is not present, because the mind is simply the questioning and formulating process. It is at precisely this timeless moment when the mind is not present, between the question and the formulation of the answer, that understanding takes place.

Therefore, if neither the question nor the formulation of the answer is present when understanding actually takes place, it cannot be said that we understand a thought. What is it then that we actually understand? Understanding understands itself. It returns us to our true nature, consciousness, which is pure intelligence. It is the answer. Understanding doesn't take place somewhere. It is our true nature.

After this timeless experience of understanding, the mind reappears with the thought, "I understood such and such." With this thought the ego is created as the supposed "understander," but the truth of our experience is that when the understanding took place, in the moment when consciousness recognized itself, the "I" was not present, the mind was not present.

We make distinctions between understanding, love, and beauty, but they are in fact all the same. Understanding is beautiful. Love is understanding. Beauty is love. Whenever we are touched by understanding, love, or beauty, it is a moment when the mind becomes naturally silent. Not silent for a long time for there is no time there. It is a timeless moment. This is the interpretation at the level of thought or reason. At the level of feeling the interpretation is that life becomes more and more fragrant.

Is there anything one can do to facilitate the understanding you are speaking of?

There is nothing the alleged separate entity can do to facilitate or prevent the understanding. This alleged entity is an object. It cannot do anything, so it should go back to sleep and leave us to have a good time. When the Self wants to make its gift to itself it creates the appropriate conditions and makes the gift. The appropriate conditions are like the wrapping paper that surrounds the gift. The gift itself is not an object.

I feel hopeless when you say there is nothing I can do about my unhappiness.

When we understand that the alleged person can do nothing, we let go of striving and in this letting go all the obstacles to happiness, at the level of thinking and feeling, are gradually revealed. Realizing that we are not an entity, we take our stand as consciousness, and allow this exposure and relaxation of the knots in the body and the mind, with loving indifference. This is the direct path, standing knowingly as consciousness under all circumstances. The gradual untangling of the knots in the body and the mind, the contractions and the beliefs, may take time. However, we start from our true nature, from a glimpse of it. We don't end with it. It is a top-down approach in which the body and the mind are gradually realigned with our experience and understanding of truth.

Often there is a glimpse of truth, followed by a sense of regret that I have been seeking for such a long time and keep getting there and losing it.

Consciousness was present as the truth seeker. To regret that consciousness was not present doesn't make any sense. Everything has always been, is, and will always be consciousness, so why worry? There is only consciousness, right this minute.

It seems that it is so simple we can't believe it. Consciousness is present all the time and the play appears within it and yet we keep sticking to the play.

And that, too, is part of the play!

If there is only consciousness, and all perceptions, sensations, and thoughts arise from and return to consciousness, are all objects an illusion?

When we say that objects are an illusion we mean that it is an illusion that objects have their own existence separate from consciousness. The experience of a separate object seems real, but the reality of this experience comes from consciousness. The object borrows its reality from consciousness. When objects are present, they are real as consciousness. They have no reality in themselves. When they are not present in consciousness, we cannot say that they exist.

However, even when we say that an object exists from the normal materialistic viewpoint, the presence of consciousness is still implied. The word "exist" means to "stand out from," so if we say that an object exists, we imply that it stands out from something else. That from which the object stands out is consciousness, that which is. It is the background. Later on, it is discovered to be the object's real nature.

The moment we understand that objects have no existence separate from consciousness, they cease to be a distraction from consciousness and become instead pointers that reveal it.

What you say makes sense intellectually but in practice I still feel that things are separate from myself. For instance I feel that this chair is separate from myself.

Touch the chair with your hands and, without interpreting your experience in any way, ask yourself if that sensation, whatever exactly it is, is separate from you, whatever you are. The answer is obviously, "No!" It is very simple. Now transpose that understanding to all your sense perceptions and ask yourself again if anything you ever experience is actually separate from yourself.

From the medical point of view, consciousness is different from what you are talking about.

Let's call that "medical consciousness." However, it is not possible to design an experiment that proves that the brain produces consciousness. If there is brain damage, for instance, we do not know that the person loses consciousness. They may have no memory or perception of external stimuli and they may have lost control of their body. If we claim, however, that the absence of these things proves that there is no consciousness, we imply that the presence of these things, by the same token, proves the existence of consciousness. If this were true, then we would have to acknowledge that a computer has consciousness, because it can record data in memory, it can record sensed data if connected to sensors and, provided with robot arms, it can move things.

34

We have no doubt that we are conscious. When we go to sleep at night, we don't receive sense impressions, we don't voluntarily control the motions of our body and we have no recollection of deep sleep. However, this does not mean that we are not present as consciousness, nor that there was a discontinuity in consciousness.

The feeling that we all have of this subjective experience of "I" will never show up on a computer screen. It is beyond the scope of science, which limits itself to the sphere of phenomena. So-called "medical consciousness" is an object; it can be observed and measured. However, true consciousness is that which observes "medical consciousness." It is that *in* which and ultimately *as* which it and all other objects appear.

Each of us *is* consciousness, and consciousness is that through which whatever we know is known. If it could be investigated as an object, it would have to be known by something else, and this "something else" would in turn be what we call consciousness.

If consciousness doesn't intervene and doesn't have preferences, why should we put Hitler in prison if he reappeared?

Consciousness welcomes the totality of the situation. By "the totality of the situation" we mean all the elements that comprise the given situation, including your own reactions. Out of this impartial welcoming, in response to the circumstances, understanding arises that may or may not lead to action. Action that flows from the totality of the situation is right action and will always be beneficial even if, in the short term, it may not appear to be effective. Action that comes from a fragment of the totality, from a separate entity, will subtly perpetuate the suffering it is trying to relieve, even if it appears beneficial in the short term, because it is itself the root cause of that suffering.

The body is involved in the world and although the witness doesn't participate in action, the body does. Even non-action is a form of action. Cowardice, for instance, is a form of action. That is the lesson that Krishna teaches Arjuna in the Bhagavad Gita. As the

Self we are the witness, but as the body, we are already involved. So just do your dharma, do what's right, do what flows from the circumstances.

Anyone who loves beauty and truth will presumably express them.

Yes, the deed that comes from the perception of beauty, truth, and love is a direct expression of beauty, truth, and love in the world. In the realm of thinking it is revealed as intelligence. In the realm of feeling it is revealed as love and joy. In the realm of perceptions it is revealed as a true work of art.

ॐ

If consciousness is fearless, why do I feel so much fear?

To be fearless implies not being afraid of death and this occurs as a result of realizing that we are that which does not die. If we are truly unafraid of death, we realize that all psychological fear is a figment of our imagination. However, in a real situation, fear may be necessary, it may be an appropriate response to a certain situation. For instance, if we were to discover a cobra in this room, fear would trigger all kinds of appropriate mechanisms. There is nothing wrong with that. It is just an appropriate response of the body-mind to a given situation. We could call this biological fear.

However, psychological fear, fear that doesn't arise out of a real situation but rather from a projection of an imaginary personal entity into a hypothetical situation in the future, is a different story. Psychological fear involves a personal entity, whereas in biological fear there is nobody who is afraid. It is inherent in the personal entity to be afraid of its own disappearance because, deep inside, we have the knowledge of the falsity of this entity.

Why is it so often said of people who have realized their true nature, that the overcoming of the fear of death brought about a dramatic change? Is it necessary for realization to happen in this way?

It is not necessary. There are innumerable ways in which consciousness can reveal itself to itself and we should not be prescriptive about it. Above all, we should not expect a particular type of experience. I once read, in an Indian text, a description by King Janaka of his enlightenment. He said, "It was a beautiful, warm night with a gentle breeze and I was in the garden of the royal palace. I was lying on my bed with my beloved. We had just made love, the birds were singing, and the fragrance of the flowers was beautiful. We were drinking delicious wine. At that moment, I heard in the distance the Brahmin chanting the Veda and I woke up."

Why do some get realization and others not?

Nobody gets realization. Our most precious treasure is freedom, and that means the freedom to be miserable if we so choose. We are free to identify with the body-mind organism if we want to. We are free to carry the baggage of the past with us or to drop it. It is very easy, but we choose not to. That's our freedom. We are freedom itself.

Why would freedom itself want to become identified?

Ask yourself the question, if such is your desire! The one who is ignorant and is willing to remain ignorant doesn't experience himself as ignorant, but as free to choose. In this freedom, he ultimately experiences happiness, because he has the freedom to think what he wants to think, to believe what he wants to believe.

When you move away from this ignorance, it is no longer a problem because you see this freedom in all human beings. You see them as this freedom, so you don't want to convert them, because nothing is a problem. You see their attachment to their beliefs, but you also see their love for their beliefs. Of course, to be attached to beliefs, to viewpoints, is misguided love, but unless they ask you a

37

question, in which case you have to answer honestly, you don't try to do anything about them, because you see that it comes from their love of freedom.

Is it the apparent person's love of freedom?

The apparent person, the separate entity, doesn't have anything. It is just a ghost. It doesn't *have* feelings; it is *made* of feelings. This apparent person, this ignorance, arises out of freedom and is also an expression of freedom. It is a very interesting, well-designed game, in which we have identified with the person and in which we have also put all the necessary signs to enable ourselves to find our way back home, sooner or later.

So ignorance is the choice of freedom and the ending of ignorance is also the choice of freedom?

Exactly. The ego, ignorance, doesn't choose anything. It gets chosen.

Can you speak of grace and conditioning?

Whatever arises out of conditioning is old. Grace is new. Whatever arises out of conditioning is simply the new packaging of an old product. Grace is truly creative. That is how to recognize what comes from grace and what is simply a continuation of the past. The continuation of the past is simply a horizontal transformation that is not a real transformation. It is an evolution. That which arises out of grace is vertical. It is a radical transformation. It brings about something new. However, it is also true to say that everything is grace. If we truly think and feel that everything is grace, then that is how we will experience the world. If we think that some things are grace and others are not, then that in turn will condition the way the world appears to us.

3

Just Say "Yes" Inside

Is there any place for devotion in this teaching of non-duality?

Yes, but the important question is "Devotion to what?" We are devoted to reality, to God, to consciousness, not to an object, a fragment, an image. We are not interested in idolatry. Devotion, as it is usually understood, is directed towards some kind of object, an image, a deity with some characteristics, a human teacher, a personal God, or to the divine qualities of a personal God. These are all objects. I am not suggesting that this kind of devotion is useless. It is useful and it eventually takes the devotee to Truth.

However, the kind of devotion that is the foundation for the search for truth is very pure. It is not tainted by images, by objectivity. It is so pure that in the beginning it is not recognized for what it is. It looks like profound interest and is both passionate and dispassionate at the same time. Passionate because there is a lot of energy that is devoted to it and dispassionate because there is no agitation.

Ultimately, all human beings are looking for the same truth. To begin with we look for it in gross objects and then in subtle objects, such as spiritual experiences. Gradually, as we come nearer the mark, we understand that the ultimate spiritual object, truth, freedom, happiness, love, is not an object.

Can the desire for happiness ever be an obstacle?

The desire for happiness comes from happiness and leads to it. However, the desire for a happy state is an obstacle. A happy state is a particular experience of the body and the mind. In such an experience the body and the mind are touched, as it were, by our true nature, by happiness, and for a brief period of time they shine with its brilliance. The brilliance belongs to consciousness, to our true nature, and not to the body or the mind, although they can express it. It is a misinterpretation of the experience of happiness to think that it comes from the body or the mind. To pursue a repeat of this experience only reinforces the misunderstanding and therefore the unhappiness.

We want a method, a trick, to enable us to surrender more.

Surrender the desire for more. At the moment of surrender, we feel a deep emotion that is the resolution of conflicts. It leaves us in a state of detachment, a natural welcoming. In the beginning, it is difficult to stay in this welcoming because we want to experience again the feelings that accompanied the moment of surrender. There is no need for this. Just stay surrendered.

If one can avoid devoting oneself to objects through the devotion to truth, to God, is it possible to see others as Godlike and see yourself in that other person as God?

By using the word God we mean the Divine, consciousness. We don't mean a personal God or a being with separate existence. The word "God" has been so misused that it is difficult to understand it without the association of previous ideas. When someone quoted to Voltaire the scripture, "God has created us in his own image," he replied, "And conversely!" A God that is like us is not the real God; it is a personal God. It is a projection of our belief of separation, a projection of the ego.

However, once we have understood that there is no experiential or rational evidence for the belief that consciousness is personal, we become naturally open to the possibility that it is impersonal and universal. We become open to the possibility that the consciousness that is seeing and understanding these words right now is the same consciousness that is experiencing everything that is being experienced by all sentient beings at this very moment. The more we test out this possibility in daily life situations the more we find that the truth of it is confirmed in our experience. When we meet a so-called other we have the deep feeling that we are one and the same consciousness. God sees God everywhere.

How does devotion to the truth develop in everyday life?

As we grow up, we look for happiness in different kinds of objects and it takes different people varying amounts of time to come to the deep understanding that what we truly want is not contained in any object, gross or subtle. As a result of this understanding we begin to search for that which is not an object, not realizing at first that seeking is always directed towards some kind of goal, some kind of subtle object.

However, sooner or later, often after an encounter with a teacher, this search will end in a glimpse of truth, a glimpse of our true nature. Once this has happened we begin to fall in love with that which is behind and beyond the mind. We become more and more interested in it and attracted by it. As this love and attraction deepen, so our attraction for objects diminishes correspondingly. However, there is no rejection of anything in this path. Our interests in life are gradually consumed in this great fire of interest in our true nature and, as a result, our previous interests fall away. They are outshone. Seeking comes to an end and true devotion takes birth.

To whom should we pray?

It is for the one who is praying to know, but a true prayer always originates from the deep feeling that there is some reality that encompasses all things, a feeling that there is a hidden harmony behind and within everything. Any prayer that originates from this deep feeling, no matter how misguided it may be, will always receive a response that will enable us to grow spiritually, in understanding, love, truth, and beauty. So when we pray, we pray to that which is. Ultimately, we pray to that which we are.

There seems to be a basic duality in the universe between myself and others. Do I discover unity by looking inward or outward?

You could go either way but the easiest way is to go inwards. When you say "myself" as opposed to "others," you superimpose a gross object, your body, or a subtle object, your mind, onto what you actually are. This shows that you have not discriminated between that which is objective, that is, the body and the mind, and that which is subjective, that which truly deserves to be called "I." In fact, even as body-minds we are not really separate. For instance, we share the air we breathe, we constantly exchange substances with the environment, and we interchange ideas with one another. However, this does not imply that there is no distinction between us. There is diversity in the gross and subtle realms.

Once we have understood that the true "I" is that in which the body, the mind, and the world appear, we can then question the true nature of this "I," the subject. For instance ask yourself, "Are there two subjects?" If the answer is, "Yes," then we have to ask ourselves what is the foundation for such a claim. We experience ourselves as one single subject, not two. What is the reality of the experience? We have a concept that there are as many subjects as there are bodies but this is simply a belief. There is nothing to substantiate it. We have inherited this belief from our conditioning. Why create many subjects if we actually only ever experience one?

This does not prove or establish the fact that there is only one subject. However, why believe that there are several subjects, if this claim is without foundation? If we take the understanding that is closest to our actual experience, that there is only one subject, everything suddenly falls into place. Life itself becomes miraculous. It becomes the living proof of that understanding. However, in order for this to happen we have to be open to the possibility that there is only one subject.

This involves a two-step process. To begin with, we inquire in this way so as to open ourselves to the possibility that there is only one subject. It is not enough to believe that this possibility is true, simply because we have been told it by our teacher or read it in a book. We have to investigate for ourselves and come to the deep understanding that there is nothing to substantiate the belief that there is more than one subject. By doing so we eliminate the obstacles in the mind, the belief systems that prevent us from even visualizing that possibility.

Once we are open to this possibility we can then take the second step, which is to begin to live our life from this point of view. In other words we begin to test it out in practice. Very soon we start to experience that it is so and our life now becomes a celebration of this understanding.

Is it simply enough to open up the mind?

That is all we can do from the vantage point of the mind. The mind cannot see consciousness.

So we shouldn't take up any position.

It is important not to take up any position, because an alternative position is simply another object, another attachment. We use this inquiry to undermine all belief systems, all attachment to concepts of any kind, and this leaves us in the absence of any position, in "not knowing." In this "not knowing" everything changes and everything becomes possible. We take a new direction that cannot be formulated but which expresses itself as a living experience of freedom and happiness.

The place of "not knowing" is the experience of the now. However, it requires understanding, not effort, to drop belief systems to which we are attached. In order to drop the belief that there are many selves, many consciousnesses, we have to start by going through the reasoning process that leads to the understanding that there is no valid argument, based on our actual experience, to suggest that consciousness is limited or personal, despite the fact that what appears in it may be so.

Subsequently, when such a belief occurs, we can either develop this reasoning again so as to remind ourselves of the understanding, or we can go directly to the center using our previous understanding, without going through the reasoning process. We have the choice. The moment we are fully convinced that the belief has no value, we drop it. At some point, this tool of reasoning has done its job. It cannot go any further. In India, it is compared to a stick that is used to stir the fire. In the end, it is thrown into the fire. It also has to burn away.

ॐ

There is a constant movement between happiness and sadness. Is it possible to just rest with the feeling of freedom and existence without having the sense "I am happy" or "I am sad"?

The feeling "I am happy" or "I am sad" perpetuates the notion of a person who is happy or sad, and this very notion is the seed of misery. To be happy as a person, as a separate entity, is a total impossibility. If we claim that we are happy, then happiness has apparently already left. When we are happy, we don't know that we are happy, because happiness requires childlike innocence. When a child is happy, he doesn't know that he is happy. He doesn't formulate it, he simply enjoys it. This is a very different situation from one in which we create an enjoyer, who we then claim is happy or unhappy.

In freedom from concepts we are this happiness. The troublemaker is the belief that we are separate. The understanding that we are the witness, consciousness, and not the body-mind, reinstates freedom. First we understand this conceptually. This intellectual understanding goes very deep and is of great value because it already contains within itself a glimpse of truth.

44

However, later on we go deeper than intellectual understanding and then we don't even need to think of it, we just are it. We become accustomed again to being that which we have always been.

Does the happiness of which you are speaking have an opposite?

The happiness that seems like the opposite of the feeling of misery is the very happiness that we call "happiness." There are not two happinesses! Happiness is our true nature. We all know happiness. When we talk about happiness, we all know what we are talking about, because we all have the experience of happiness. Similarly, we all know what the word "consciousness" or "I" refers to. The problem is that we make happiness an object that comes and goes and then create its counterpart, a personal entity, which owns and loses this happiness. We make this happiness, which is our permanent nature, into an intermittent object. It is just a misunderstanding, a false perspective. All that needs to be done is to restore the correct perspective and then gradually everything else is corrected.

When we say, "I am this" or "I am that," it is always a mistake. We are not "this" or "that." We are both nothing and everything. It is not true to say, "I am sad." We should say instead, "At this moment a feeling of sadness is flowing through me." If we just let the feeling of sadness flow, we automatically and unknowingly take our stand in that which is not flowing. In order to be aware of the movement of whatever is flowing, we take our stand unknowingly, naturally, and spontaneously as the presence in which it appears. In fact that is the only way to take our stand as this presence. This presence is not an object, so any effort towards this presence would make us take our stand in an artificial place, as an object. However, by letting everything flow we simply find ourselves as that which we truly are.

The thought, "I am sad" creates the false "I," and the false "I," at that moment, has no existence apart from this thought. This thought is itself witnessed by the true "I" who is enjoying the show. All we can say from the vantage point of the mind is that "I" is never experienced as being limited. All we can say is that there is consciousness and nothing else. Only consciousness is certain. The

45

witness that we are talking about is the ultimate witness. It is not an object. An objective witness is a creation of the mind. It is simply a concept. When we talk about the witness we are talking of this "I,'" consciousness, understanding these words right now. It is immediate. Truth is one hundred percent certain.

What do you mean by an objective witness?

In the Advaita or non-dual tradition one of the tools that is used is the discrimination between the perceiver and the perceived. We take our stand as that which sees, the witness, not that which is seen. However, this understanding is incomplete. It is useful because it enables us to take a step back from our objective experience towards the source, to release our firm hold on objects. However, in this case there is still the possibility that this witness may be personal. We therefore have to go further back and understand that the true witness is that which can never be described or experienced as an object, in which all objects, including the objective witness, the apparently personal witness, appear.

What is self-confidence and how does it develop?

Self-confidence is trust in the Self. The more we test the truth of what is being spoken about here, the more our trust in it develops. If we simply keep this understanding at the conceptual level it will remain merely an interesting notion. It has no practical impact unless we apply it in our daily lives. That is how we become more and more convinced about truth. We test it out in our lives. The more we do this, the more we find that this conviction is confirmed in all realms of our lives by love, justice, and beauty. It is not just confirmed in the rational realm by intelligence.

Does this understanding imply a life without pain or tragedy?

This understanding implies a life without psychological suffering. There is no tragedy, really. There may be tragedy in the "story" of our lives, but in truth, there is no tragedy happening to us. Ultimately, the story is only there to teach us this distinction. The moment we take the lesson, even the story changes to reveal itself as beauty, love, and intelligence. Do not be attached to the concept that misery is unavoidable. As long as we are attached to this concept, there will be misery.

However, pain is physical and unavoidable. Nor indeed is it desirable to avoid all pain. Pain triggers all sorts of bodily mechanisms that protect the body from injury.

It may take an unknown amount of time to dispel ignorance.

If you believe this, it will postpone the dissolution of ignorance. Be happy now. Be free now. Don't postpone anything. reality appears in accordance with your desire. We become whatever we think about. Allow yourself to be happy in all realms of your existence. There is nothing to be gained by being a starving artist. Allow yourself to be in celebration. Do not restrict yourself. If you find that you do, then be aware that you are not allowing yourself to be happy. The Self, that which you are, is pure happiness, and it is infinite, without boundaries. Don't put any restrictions on it. Don't think, "I want to be happy in this particular way." Just be completely open to the possibility of being happy in all realms of your life and leave it up to God to choose how. Just say "Yes" inside. That's all it takes.

What is the content of mind and the function of thought?

When we say the "content of mind," we mean thoughts and images. The mind is a bag full of thoughts and images. However, on closer scrutiny, it turns out there is no bag. The bag itself is just one more thought. There is no mind other than the concept of mind. There is thinking and imagining but nobody has ever experienced the mind in the way that it is normally conceived of, as a container of thoughts and images, so why claim that there is such a mind? However, we are certain that there is consciousness, presence, and that all thoughts and images appear within it.

When we use the term mind therefore, we usually refer to this thinking and imagining process. The function of mind is to create. It is a tool to survive. It is also a tool to find happiness and to celebrate it. For a certain period of time, its purpose is to approach the truth, to think about the truth, to explore and investigate.

47

Higher reasoning uses the mind as a tool to clear up the confusion. However, at a certain point there is no more need of this type of reasoning. Only celebration remains, and it is expressed according to one's skills, tendencies, and God-given talents. That is the proper use of the mind.

Improper use of the mind is to dwell in misery, in negative thinking. Negative thinking always originates from the position, "I am a person," "I am a body-mind." This type of thinking has to be uprooted through understanding. The understanding process is very easy. When you think, "I am a person," ask yourself, "Is it really true? What am I? Am I the body, am I the mind, or am I consciousness in which they appear?"

We cannot understand merely by thinking but that doesn't imply that we have to stop thinking. Thinking is not a problem the moment we welcome it, the moment we just allow the flow of thoughts without any interference.

We are not the I-thought or the I-feeling. We are that in which the I-thought, the I-feeling, and all the thoughts, feelings, and perceptions of all sentient beings, past, present, and future, in this universe and all universes, in all dimensions, appear. When we understand that thoughts are not a problem, then the confusion is already being cleaned up.

Why was the confusion made in the first place?

For animation purposes. Diversity is beautiful. Consciousness likes to live at the extreme of all its possibilities. However, that answer is only partially true. It is a concession to the mind that is trying to understand something it can never understand. When this is understood, we no longer ask the question.

The reason that the question "Why?" cannot be satisfactorily answered by the mind is that inherent in the question is the idea of cause and effect. "Why this?" "Because of that." The idea of cause and effect is itself a creation of the mind and cannot therefore be used to investigate the nature of the mind's confusion. It would be like a thief investigating a robbery. We would not be able to rely on the outcome!

4

The Mother of All Problems

If I put my foot on the floor, there is a sensation of resistance. Does this create the sense of separation?

It is not the experience of resistance that creates the sense of separation. It is our interpretation of the experience. The interpretation of the experience is responsible for the creation of the apparently external objects, that is, our foot and the floor. However, our actual experience is simply a sensation of resistance. In fact it is not even an experience of resistance. It is simply a sensation, a neutral, nameless sensation. This experience itself is felt inside us. However, our interpretation creates the apparent "outside." The outside is always a concept. The experience is always inside. Therefore, at the level of experience there is no outside. There is no separation at the level of experience. Separation is always a concept that appears after the experience.

We have created feelings, contractions, and localizations in the body that make us feel we are separate. They seem to make separation an actual experience. If we take a closer look and fully welcome this feeling of separation, we see that it doesn't actually separate anything from anything. Separation has no reality. It is never actually experienced. It has an apparent reality as long as it remains in a twilight zone, which means when it is only partially seen.

When there is no sense of separation, there is still a sense of "I am" as a perception.

This sense of "I am" that you refer to is located in the body as a sensation. It is a bodily sensation that appears to you, consciousness. The small "I" is that which appears. The real "I" is that in which it appears. That which appears is limited in time and space; it has some sort of contour. That in which it appears is limitless. The small "I" and the real "I" coexist, but not at the same level. The small "I" cannot exist independently of the real "I," but the real "I" exists independently of the small "I." Their natures are different, although ultimately the real nature of the small "I," whether it is a thought or a feeling, is nothing other than consciousness, the real "I." The small "I" is perceived, the real "I" perceives.

Whatever is being experienced is not you. It is enough to simply see whatever is being experienced clearly and impartially. By seeing in this way we are already taking our stand in our true nature. For example, we don't have to formulate, "I am not this perception." To fully perceive our body liberates us from being the body.

It is important not to expect anything. To want a divine experience of pleasure on top of freedom is the "fall" from our problem-free nature. This problem-free nature is joyful and peaceful. It is not something that comes and goes. There is a sense of freedom, a perfume. What really matters is that which is permanent. People often say that this experience comes and goes. If it does, it is not what we are talking about here. Whatever is impermanent must be objective.

If I categorize emotions as negative and want to get rid of them, I inflame them. There are moments when I can see that they are not me and can let go of them. However, because I am not established in knowing that they are not what I am, they keep on catching me again and again.

There are two mistakes in your question. The first is to take yourself for someone who is not established and who might become established in the future. This someone will never become established in the future. This someone will never become established. The second is the desire to change things, the judging and condemnation of whatever appears.

The moment we condemn a feeling as "bad," we want to get rid of it. Who wants to get rid of it? The one who wants to get rid of it is the one who creates it. The one who wants to get rid of anger is itself angry about being angry. It will never come to an end unless you see the process. It is like a madman who continues to bang his head against the wall until he realizes what is going on. This refusal is very deeply rooted in us and, as we become more and more interested in this perspective, it reveals itself in all kinds of ways. However, behind all of these faces there is one single sense of being a person, of separation: the I-thought.

There is strong sense of the I-thought connected with watching. There is a reflection of the "I" in the mind. It is connected with the heart center. The more attention it receives, the more the trouble.

This connection is a perceived object. Even the heart center is an object, a perception that comes and goes, a limitation. It is not a problem. The reflection of the "I" in the mind is a thought, the I-thought. At the level of feeling it is a bodily sensation, the I-feeling. These are all objects that come and go. They appear and disappear within that which never appears or disappears, their source. It is for this reason that, on the path of self-inquiry, we do not look for feelings, we look for their source. We don't stop with the I-thought or I-feeling. We let them merge with their source, which is the subject, consciousness. That is the true "I."

This true "I" is not itself a perception or a thought. It is too close to be perceived. We can only perceive something that is at an apparent distance. That which is at a zero distance from the

51

perceiving reality can never be perceived. For instance, the eye can never perceive itself. It can perceive its reflection in a mirror or its image on a photograph, but it can never perceive itself because it is at a zero distance from itself. It is the same with consciousness. It can never perceive itself as an object. It can only be itself. When consciousness tries to perceive itself, it creates an object, and that object is the I-thought or the I-feeling.

The I-thought is not a problem as long as it refers to consciousness. When it becomes attached to an attribute, to a noun or an adjective, such as "I am a woman," "I am a human being," "I am happy," "I am unhappy," "I am frustrated," and so on, it becomes the mother of all problems.

೮ঽ

In meditation, as thoughts subside and the feelings that fuel them become apparent, it is clear that the impulse to think sometimes arises in order to avoid the discomfort of this mass of undifferentiated feelings. However, unlike thoughts, these feelings tend to grow rather than subside when welcomed.

Don't welcome the feelings themselves; welcome the totality of your experience. The fact that you speak of this "mass of undifferentiated feeling" suggests that you have already differentiated them from the rest of your experience. You are focusing on them. You are involved in a relationship with them, with one aspect of the totality of your experience. The reason you focus on this mass of feelings is due to a subtle desire to get rid of them. However, the more you focus on the feelings, the more you aggravate them. The more you scratch, the more they itch. Stop scratching!

The scratching comes from a desire to get rid of the itching. Welcome the itching, but don't try to do anything about it. See that you are focusing onto it. The fact that it is experienced as uncomfortable implies that you are resisting it, you are reacting against it. You have superimposed a feeling of resistance onto the original feeling. This is the feeling of anger towards the feeling of anger. In this way, layers of feeling are built up one on top of another. See the game that is being played. The moment we see the game, we stop playing, and everything gradually goes back to normal, layer after layer.

There are, however, some practical tools you can use, at least for a while. For instance, when you feel hypnotized by a feeling in your body, downgrade the feeling to the level of a sensation. A feeling is a bodily sensation attached to the concept of being a person, a separate entity. See clearly that this separate entity doesn't exist, that it is not the subject, the "feeler" of the feeling. It is simply a thought. Seeing this clearly enables the thought, the I-thought, to be dropped spontaneously. Divested of its psychological content, the feeling is now experienced simply as a sensation in the body. Explore it and discover that it is just a neutral sensation arising in your presence. It is not a problem. If it has nothing new to teach you, leave it and move on.

Sometimes as a result of our residual desire to go somewhere, to achieve, there is a tendency to artificially create this mass of sensations in order to remain busy getting rid of it. However, the more we want to get rid of them, the more we create them. It is a "loop" of residual activity. Don't try to get rid of something that you have created, just stop creating it and understand that it is your very desire to get rid of it that perpetuates it.

I have trouble with the word "welcome." "Receive" seems more appropriate.

"Accept" is also OK. The important thing is to welcome the totality of the situation. Don't welcome the object, which is just one aspect of your current experience, welcome the totality. If we remain hypnotized by a problem, by a negative element, we are not welcoming the totality of the situation, we are focusing on one aspect of it. True welcoming is always the welcoming of the totality.

I sometimes feel that even welcoming is an avoidance of being.

Artificial welcoming, intentional welcoming, is welcoming that has a personal goal in mind, and in this sense, it could be said that it is an avoidance of being. However, true welcoming is not an avoidance of anything. To reveal feelings in full light involves seeing feelings clearly for what they are. Let these feelings be purified of any psychological content in this welcoming space. When we look at a cloud in the sky, the cloud has no psychological content, no feeling of "me" attached to it.

As long as you understand this welcoming as an activity, don't do it. As long as there is a doer, a person doing it, don't do it. However, there are many things we do without doing them as a person. They are in fact being done. For instance, when we breathe, *we* don't breath. When a thought comes to us, *we* don't think it. It just comes to us. It is in this way that welcoming takes place.

In fact, welcoming is not an activity. It may appear to be so in the beginning, because it seems that a certain effort is required to allow, rather than reject, certain unpleasant aspects of our experience. However, as we become more established in welcoming, we realize that welcoming involves the *cessation* of the activity of resistance, rather than the initiation of any further activity. It is the allowing of everything that appears within the field of consciousness just to be as it is.

To begin with welcoming is usually understood as something that we do. Later on it is understood to be something that we stop doing. It is understood as the cessation of resistance, of exclusively focusing onto a fragment of our experience. And finally welcoming is understood to be what we are, the natural, loving, open space in which all things come into being, abide, and dissolve.

Surrender to not knowing. Understand that every time that you have been happy in your life it came out of nowhere in an unpredictable way. We cannot secure happiness through knowing or doing. Let go of this waste of energy. Things will still be accomplished but the agitation comes to an end. Then, whenever we do something we enjoy it because there is no effort. We are not involved as a person and life becomes a celebration.

54

I am often uncertain whether I am involved as a person or not.

The way to find out whether the "person" is involved is to see whether the activity is motivated by a desire to achieve something exclusively for yourself as a person. To make sure that it is impersonal, that it is in harmony with the totality, ask yourself if you would approve of the action if you were an all-knowing, benevolent judge. This will immediately give you the impersonal, impartial point of view.

For instance if you take good care of your body, you may think that such a concern is personal. However, if you look at it from the vantage point of an all-knowing and benevolent judge, taking good care of the body which has been placed in her care, you discover that such an activity is not necessarily personal. The body and mind are tools for celebration and the all-knowing, benevolent judge wants the celebration to take place. On the other hand, let us suppose that you have a thought of getting even with someone. From the point of view of the all-knowing and benevolent judge, she wants the thought to be dropped and for you to be happy. This type of activity is usually personal.

Discriminate between impersonal, spontaneous deeds and those that are personal. Don't worry when there are moments when you are not sure. It is enough if you have tried with goodwill to apply this in your life. In such a case, your intention to take the impersonal stand is already the impersonal stand. Just do your best. Whatever comes out of this willingness to be impersonal will be impersonal, even if you make a mistake. It is the very willingness to be impersonal that seals the impersonality of your deed.

಄

From this place of unknowing do you lose the feeling of existence?

No, you don't lose the feeling of existence. You are existence itself.

Even though I understand that I am not separate, I still feel separate at the physical level.

Ignorance at the conceptual level is thinking that reinforces the idea that one is a body-mind. Ignorance at the level of the body involves feelings that make us feel we are separate, that we are this body-mind entity, that we have been created. These feelings trigger the personal I-thought.

When such feelings appear we should welcome the totality of the situation of which they are a part. When this has been completely welcomed, the attention is free to go elsewhere. We know that welcoming is complete when the situation has nothing new to teach us, when it becomes repetitive. Perhaps we can give the situation a few more moments to make sure we have looked at it from all sides. If there is no further unfolding and the feeling remains, we should ask ourselves whether we could live with this feeling for the rest of our life. If we do not want to get rid of it, if we could live with it forever, it means that it is no longer a problem; it no longer has the capacity to make us feel separate. However, if we want to get rid of the feeling, we must see that this desire arises out of another feeling, a feeling of aversion, of resistance.

Each time a feeling is completely welcomed, it loses its separating power. It becomes neutralized. Another layer of deeper and subtler feeling will now arise, and should be welcomed in the same way. Layer after layer of feelings come to the surface in this way and gradually, without our knowing it, the stronghold of the ego is exposed and dissolved.

Two things may happen in this welcoming: if we stay with a feeling and completely welcome the totality of the situation, it will lead us upstream to the I-thought which is in turn reabsorbed in the source. At this point the fear of disappearing, the fear of death, the underlying existential fear, vanishes for good.

However, there may also be localized feelings that have no psychological counterpart in the I-thought. When we see these feelings for what they are, simply a perpetuation of the agitation, and have circumscribed them and realized that they have nothing new to teach us, we just drop them. In the case of such feelings we learn the skill of dropping them earlier and earlier, and they appear less and less frequently. They lose their energy as we ignore them. We just recognize them for what they are. At some point, they will not bother us any longer. It is similar to someone giving up smoking. During the first few days, he has the desire to smoke every ten seconds or so. After two weeks, the desire will only show up once every five minutes and, after ten years, it won't show at all. There is a gradual spacing out of these feelings.

When the feelings are "good," it is not so easy to just leave them.

Good feelings are to be enjoyed. They are the expression of joy and take us back to joy, which is our true nature. Just enjoy them; be one with them. Understand that a moment of happiness comes from grace, and this moment of happiness is teaching us that happiness is not in an object. We have to know that we are this happiness in the moment. The object is almost irrelevant. The object is part of the dream but the happiness is real. Therefore, let go of the object. Surrender the object. Causeless joy is self-explanatory. If we are looking for it, we won't find it, but when we stop looking for it, it finds us.

You suggested staying in clear seeing and in not knowing. I escape from that by formulating, for example, "I am consciousness."

In the beginning, this type of thought takes us to the experience of our true nature, so it is not a problem. However, after a while it becomes shorter and shorter and at some point, we don't even need to take the thought. We go directly to the experience, to the knowing inside, to the place we love the most, and we stay there. At some point, the need for this thought disappears because we find a more direct way to go back to our true nature. This thought is not an obstacle; it is a vehicle.

You once mentioned a sense of wholeness that later becomes holiness. Could you expand on this?

A sense of wholeness comes when we feel that everything is inside us. When we feel that, we understand that everything is our own emanation, an emanation from consciousness. This understanding compels everything that is experienced to unveil itself, to reveal its true nature. This unveiling is the revelation of the sacred.

When we truly feel that the universe is in us, *is* us, that there is no separation, that there is this wholeness, then the universe and the events in the world unfold in accordance with this perspective, which is the true perspective. They reveal the sanctity, the holiness of the world. They reveal the permanent miracle. First it is experienced as a feeling and later on, it is confirmed by our experience of the world.

I often find myself daydreaming.

Daydreaming is an avoidance of the now which is deemed to be boring. It is an escape from whatever is arising in the moment and it takes us into the past or the future. It relates to the thought that we are a personal entity.

There is a difference between daydreaming and what we could call "free thinking." Daydreaming could be called "captive thinking" in the sense that it is captive of the notion that we are a person, that there is someone to whom the daydream is happening, a projected someone. In "free thinking," thoughts arise freely and there can be strange associations, but there is no entity around which they revolve. It is very creative.

It is also necessary to have practical thoughts, for instance to make plans, to book the car into the garage, to make a shopping list, and so on. There is nothing wrong with these types of thoughts. They are an appropriate response to the current situation and do not need to hinge around a separate entity.

There is another type of thinking that doesn't depend on, create, or maintain the idea of a separate entity and these are thoughts about truth. They come from the truth and lead us back to it. We could call it "higher reasoning." It is only the first type of thinking, which revolves around a separate entity, that leads to misery.

However, even if we understand that something is a waste of energy, we may still keep doing it for a while. For instance, if a smoker understands that smoking is detrimental to his health, he may not give it up straight away; it may take some time. This doesn't mean that the understanding is not there. If, from the fact that daydreaming is present, you infer that there is no understanding, you are judging yourself. Having understood, realize that any understanding that is not applied is sterile. This delay in putting your understanding into practice is your decision. You can apply it immediately or postpone it.

If we drop a daydream, then the next time one appears, we will become conscious of it earlier. Each time we do this it becomes easier to drop it the next time, so the average duration of a daydream will get shorter and shorter. At some point, we no longer daydream because, before it takes root, we catch the impulse to avoid the now, which triggers the daydreaming in the first place. At this point the understanding, the moment of becoming aware of the daydreaming, and the moment of dropping it are simultaneous.

You have spoken of our non-acceptance of the simplicity or ordinariness of the now. I think that for enlightenment to take place, the now must become very special.

This rejection of the now means that you have not yet understood that objects have nothing to offer in terms of happiness. Whatever objects are present are labeled insufficient, in terms of their capacity to bring about happiness, and therefore there is a craving for new objects. This process maintains the ego. It is only when we are truly indifferent to objects that we can be in the now. When we are in the now, the true nature of objects is revealed. They are revealed as a permanent miracle because there are no objects as such.

I feel that you are responsible for the stillness that I feel at the moment.

My presence is your presence. Just let go of the notion that your presence is not my presence. It is our presence. There's no difference, because when we come here, all of us as individuals, each of us is a component of the celebration. It seems that everything is being spoken from this mouth, but we are in fact all one huge body and somehow this mouth is, for the time being, the mouthpiece of this huge body. However, we are this one body and it is important for the ears not to feel separate from the mouth. We are one huge universe speaking and listening to itself.

This distinction between student and teacher is an obstacle. Don't indulge it. It is much simpler if, in accordance with our understanding that there is one single consciousness, we see these meetings simply as an opportunity to experience and celebrate this oneness, rather than hoping we are going to get something from someone. We celebrate it in silence, through our relationships, through our conversations, through our activities, and so on. We are all already perfectly equipped for happiness.

Can you say something about the relationship with the teacher?

When a truth seeker approaches a teacher, it is almost inevitable that he or she will take the teacher as a person to begin with. However, the teacher is like a vacuum, a silent empty space. There is nobody there. Therefore this projection from the truth seeker gets no support. It is like trying to catch a slippery fish. We come away empty-handed.

As a result of the lack of support for the personal entity, the student begins to feel the presence of a loving, impersonal friendliness that arises in relation to the teacher. This is the experience of the real nature that we all share. Often we first experience this in the company of the teacher and this then becomes the model for all our other relationships.

The response that does come from the teacher is not directed towards the person. It is directed towards consciousness, the real nature of the truth seeker. It is a movement from consciousness to consciousness. It is a movement within consciousness. The truth seeker may not be aware of this. In fact he may feel that he is being addressed as a person. However, even if the answer is taken at the personal level, a seed will have been sown in the back of the truth seeker's mind. In due course this seed will sprout, and a process of higher reasoning will begin. This in turn will lead the student to the understanding that the teacher is not a person. From this point on it is this impersonal friendliness that the teacher and the student share that becomes both the means and the expression of the teaching.

The word impersonal suggests something so distant and unintimate to me.

By "impersonal" I simply mean not based on the thought or feeling that we are a separate person. It is this thought and feeling that actually prevents true intimacy and lovingness. Whenever we love, we disappear as a person.

When we say that the teacher is impersonal or that there is nobody there, we are not implying that the teacher is without a character or that he is not animated. Not at all. We simply mean that the thoughts, feelings, and activities of such a teacher do not hinge around the notion of being a separate entity.

ᘓ

When I get stuck in my head I let it go and move into my body and then the "stuckness" in the head goes. Is this a "doing"?

It depends what you mean by "letting it go." If it is spontaneous, in other words if there is no doer of the action, if it is the silence that, without any will or intervention on your behalf, gradually permeates your body, that is one thing. On the other hand, if you somehow channel silence through your body, that is a different story. The mind can create all kinds of strange states, especially when we reach deep levels of relaxation.

The silence that is referred to here is not the silence of the mind. It is the presence of consciousness. It is always present, even in the presence of thoughts, feelings, and bodily activity. It is behind and beyond all the states of dreaming, sleeping, and waking. This silence is not objective, it is not perceived. It is that which perceives. It is known as consciousness, "beingness," or "I am-ness," and later on as happiness, love, and beauty.

We should just let everything that is objective flow, almost without noticing it. We should be indifferent to all states, including states of the body. You may go through states in which not only your mind is silent and your body transparent, but also your body is totally expanded and full of light, and it can be very pleasurable. However, even if that happens, it is still a state in the body; it is still something that has a beginning and an end. It comes and goes, so it's not worth a penny!

5

Don't Leave the Throne

You spoke of there being nothing to do, no desire for great experience. Later, I was playing music with friends and afterwards there was a profound stillness. It seemed as though the practice of attending to the beat and rhythm brought about this stillness. I find that not doing or not looking for anything is so intangible, especially in the light of such an experience.

When you were in that stillness, did you have any goal?

No.

This absence of working towards a goal is what is meant by non-doing. It doesn't mean that the body or the mind is not active. Non-doing simply refers to the absence of striving. When we are in the now, devoid of any intention, the happiness that is inherent in our true nature reveals itself. When we focus our attention on some kind of activity the mind moves away from the past and the future, from thinking, and we are completely present to the experience. At some point, the objective aspect of the experience loses its attraction, because ultimately bodily sensations are boring. Then, that which is always in the background and between the beats reveals itself as stillness, as peace.

It is important to understand this process, to understand that playing music hasn't in any way caused the stillness. If you think that this stillness is derived from playing music then, the next time you play, it won't appear. This peace is causeless. The causeless is beautiful because it is entirely independent of circumstances. We can have it everywhere because we are always the same, everywhere. It is natural.

Stop thinking that you are a beggar. However, it is useless just to think, "I am a king." We have to understand who we are and *discover* that we are the king. Merely to think it is a superimposition. Be open to the possibility that you are without limit, that consciousness is infinite, beyond space and time.

If we think that consciousness is within, and by "within" we mean within the mind, we shrink the experience and it vanishes. It loses its perfume of infinity. It is "within" in the sense that it has an intimate quality of "I-am-ness," but on the other hand it contains everything within itself. This is what Pascal meant when he said that its center is everywhere and its circumference nowhere. After the experience of our true nature, we shrink it by thinking that "I" as a person had the experience. That eclipses it. Don't think, "I had the experience," but rather, "I am the experience."

Although there is nobody that can do anything about the understanding, at the same time, samsara just seems to continue. So the understanding seems to be lacking.

Don't give up easily to samsara. Don't let samsara lure you into thinking that there is samsara. It is only if you *think* that there is samsara that there is samsara. Don't accept it. You are always the Self. Don't leave the throne. However, if you want to leave the throne, you are free to do so because you are the king and the king can do as he pleases.

64

It seems to require an effort, because it appears that we are pushed off the throne. In this situation there is a delicate balance between not reacting and watching.

Yes, but see that it is your freedom. Understand that if the king wants to play beggars, the entire court is going to play along and kick the king, just to please him!

But the king is thinking, "I wish I wasn't playing a beggar."

To play the beggar is to identify with the body and the mind. The identification with the body-mind creates the beggar. If we think we are this body-mind, we are playing beggars, but we don't have to. There is samsara only if we identify with the body-mind. From the vantage point of the Self, there is only a beautiful display of energies. There is of course absolutely nothing wrong with the body-mind. On the contrary, it is a beautiful tool of celebration. It is only our exclusive identification with it that makes us feel like beggars.

Too often the beggar is the starting point.

The feeling of being a beggar cannot appear without consciousness, no matter how wretched the feeling. Consciousness was present before the feeling of being a beggar appeared. It is present during the feeling and it is present when the feeling vanishes. Therefore, consciousness is the starting point, not the beggar.

We are this awareness which is not an object. We are that in which this body-mind and all other body-minds, all other objects, appear. We are much bigger than a body-mind. Keep returning to this understanding.

A time comes when we no longer need to question the validity of feeling and knowing that we are not the body-mind. Whenever the image or the thought that we are the body-mind appears, we drop it immediately because we know that it is not the truth. Whenever we have doubts, we can go back to the understanding that we are the awareness in which all objects, including the body-mind, appear. Reason alone is not sufficient to stabilize us in this experience. We also need to *feel* that we are not the body-mind.

In order to feel that we are not the body-mind, we have to investigate the true nature of the body, and this is done by welcoming bodily sensations. It is not enough to assume that the body is an object, or simply to think it. We have to have the *experience* that the body is an object. All feelings, all bodily sensations are completely allowed in this contemplation. Allowing them to be as they are, without interference, reveals the space in which they appear and, as a result, we no longer stick to them. When we are no longer tied to them in this way they are free to unfold and dance. Also, since we are not rigidly tied to them, they do not take us with them in their ups and downs. We are the changeless background and they can dance. As long as we think that we are one of them, they will take us with them wherever they go.

We have to include the body, our feelings, in our meditation. When we find ourselves immersed in the world of objects, we have to pause and try to discover what is at the origin of this chain of thoughts and feelings. Eventually we find a very subtle feeling in the body. It is not a big thing. This feeling triggers the thought that I am separate, from which desires and fears originate. These desires and fears generate tensions and contractions in the body. However, the origin of the feeling of separation is very subtle and inconspicuous. This I-feeling in its nakedness is like nothing. It vanishes easily.

This subtle I-feeling seems to require no effort to maintain itself. Is it a question of resting, waiting, surrendering?

Who is waiting? That which is expected to vanish is that which is waiting. As long as there is waiting, how could it vanish? In true surrender there is nobody surrendering. True surrendering is not an activity. If we decide to surrender, it is an activity. It is the opposite of surrender. That is why any activity, any doing on the path, ultimately doesn't work. We should surrender our surrendering. That is accomplished when we see clearly that we are still in expectation. Expectation is a subtle rejection of the now. The ego is a lie based on this rejection. In the now there is no room for the ego. The ego is always in the past or in the future. It vanishes when we come to the now.

We are in fact in the now all the time. We cannot have any perception without it. All perceiving takes place in the now. The same applies to thinking and feeling. We have many moments during the day without the troublemaker, the I-thought. However, even when the troublemaker is present, this thinking itself takes place in the now. We are always in our true nature.

In understanding a natural detachment takes place. When we try to understand who we are, what the nature of the universe is, how it appears and where it exists, our interest is dispassionate. There is no psychological interest, no person with a vested interest.

How do I find out who I am?

We find out who we are through the progressive discovery of what we are not. Once we have completely uncovered what we are not, the diamond of what we are shines. We don't need to make it shine, but we have to eliminate the beliefs and the feelings that we are a body-mind. The way to eliminate them is to contemplate them in a disinterested way. The very act of contemplation distances us from them and reveals the fact that we are not them.

We have to discover that we are peace, happiness, and fearlessness, that we are eternal. We don't have to do anything to discover it. The diamond shines by itself. This becomes self-evident when we surrender the notion that we are a person, a body-mind. It is not something that we have to do. Contemplation may seem like a doing to begin with, but in fact it is the opposite. It is the complete absence of doing, in which all residual doing is revealed layer by layer.

The feeling that I am the body-mind is so strong.

Fall in love with the void, the emptiness of the now, which makes everything possible, which has room for everything. Fall in love with the infinite mirror, with the "I am." Everything else, feelings, perceptions and thoughts, are the packaging, the box. The emptiness is the diamond inside, transparent, luminous, rare, priceless, but ever-present.

In the beginning we are hypnotized by the beauty of the box, by the colors. That's fine. Take time to contemplate the box. When our eyes get bored they revert to the diamond. When we look inside the box, we don't see the diamond at first. We see the white satin, an absence of color, but this is still the box. The diamond is transparent. That is why we fail to see it at first. We see through it to the white satin. Later we see the diamond.

When we remove the diamond from the box, we see the colors of the box through it and reflected within it. It is not because the diamond is transparent that we cannot see it. It is because we are the diamond. Everything we see is the box. The box only enhances the diamond, showcases the diamond, celebrates the diamond. Everything at every moment, the entire universe, celebrates the diamond.

Could you say more about contemplation not being an activity?

Contemplation is our true nature. It is what we are, not what we do. To contemplate means to take our stand in our true nature. Right this minute, sounds, words, sentences, understandings come to us effortlessly. Everything comes to us effortlessly. Consciousness is not something we have the freedom to turn on and off. It is on all the time. We are effortlessly aware. This effortless awareness is contemplation. It is not personal.

That which sees the person is beyond the person. That which sees the body, the mind, and the world is not of the nature of the body, the mind, or the world. That which sees all things is not a thing. To treat it as a thing is a lack of respect. To understand that it is not a thing is to put it back on the shrine. To see it as a thing is the "fall." To understand that it is not a thing is the "redemption."

We are talking about something awesome. We are saying that whatever it is that is seeing and understanding these words right now is divine consciousness itself. This doesn't mean that "I" as a body-mind am understanding these words and therefore "I" as a body-mind am divine consciousness itself. That would be the "fall" again.

Since we are not independent entities with volition and free will, why did Ramana Maharshi suggest that we ask ourselves, "Who am I?"

When Ramana Maharshi suggested asking, "Who am I?" he meant us to find the source of the I-thought and the I-feeling. The question is, to whom was he saying that? The simplistic answer would be that it was to the one who was asking the question, to the one who thought that he or she was not the source. For this one it sounded like a suggestion to do something, to practice self-inquiry.

However, the sage speaks simultaneously at different levels. In practicing self-inquiry, the mind has a bone to chew on. The mind becomes quiet as it works on the bone. In this relative quietness of the mind, whatever Ramana Maharshi said had the room, the space, and the opening to penetrate deeper to the listening presence in the heart.

When he said, "See who you are," he was not talking to the person. He was apparently talking to the person, but in fact he was talking to this beautiful consciousness, saying, "See who you are. You are myself. You are this beauty, this intelligence, this consciousness."

The action that comes from truth is efficient at many levels simultaneously. Sometimes we are told something and understand it immediately at one level, but we have a strange feeling of depth when it is said and it remains with us. Sometime later, after a few minutes or a few years, it explodes like a time bomb. If you want to practice self-inquiry when you feel that you are separate, then do so. Ask yourself, "Who feels separate?" This will lead to the higher understanding that you are this consciousness. Then there is no need to practice self-inquiry, just enjoy life and be happy. Therefore, practice self-inquiry only when you feel something is missing. When you feel happiness just rejoice. Know that it comes from your true nature, give thanks, and celebrate. That's all!

We can travel on the path of the individual, the truth seeker, practicing and seeking and, in parallel, on the path of the truth lover for whom there is no need to do anything. We can move back and forth from one path to the other. More and more, we remain as a truth lover and forget the truth seeker.

What is the prerequisite for meditation?

There are two prerequisites for meditation: one relates to the intention and the other relates to the attention.

Our intention has to be directed towards the impersonal, towards the divine. The intention to get rid of a problem, to solve a psychological issue, to acquire powers, or to become healthy, is not the kind required for meditation. Such an intention inhibits meditation. To check your motive, ask yourself, "What am I really looking for? What do I really want?" You will find the answer in the privacy of your own heart. If the intention is for anything less than the divine, for less than that which is beyond all limitations, there won't be meditation. However, if there is such an intention, meditation is already at hand. It is potentially there.

That is where the second prerequisite applies. For meditation to become actualized, our attention has to be free from any object. However, there is no possibility of liberating our attention from objects if the intention is not pure. If the intention is not pure there will always be a fixation onto something, a fear or a desire, a personal involvement. However, if the intention is pure, all that is required for the attention to liberate itself from objects is to simply notice its fixation on any object.

This fixation of the attention can take place within any one of the three realms of experience: the external world, the thoughts, and the bodily sensations or feelings. For instance, if you discover that a thought is running in circles, that would be a fixation in the mind. If you notice that your attention is drawn outside towards sounds, that would be a fixation on an external object. These two kinds of fixations are usually easy to notice and after a while we no longer indulge them. However, the third kind, the fixation on a bodily sensation, is a habit that has stronger and deeper roots for most of us. It is harder to detect because it is sometimes mistaken for stillness or peace.

We often seem to reach a place of stillness in meditation. However, although it is a quiet place, it has no juice, no perfume. If we look closer we see that the mind is in fact resting on a bodily sensation, a localization in the body.

Don't let your mind rest upon any object. In this sense, meditation requires a kind of vigilance. The only place to rest is the Self. When we create a sensation in the body to rest on, we create a pseudo Self, a pseudo "me." As soon as we detect such a pattern, we are free. When you become aware of such a localization or attachment, try to make a deliberate effort to move the attention away from it. We do this simply by allowing the sensation upon which we were resting to expand into the surrounding space or by

71

just going back to unlocalized presence. Although our mind doesn't know where unlocalized presence is, our presence knows very well where to find itself. It is always right here.

Meditation has nothing to do with eliminating the bodily sensation upon which we are resting. It is simply to notice that we are resting on it. When we try to release our attention from the object, the sensation, we notice a web of resistance that keeps us attached to it. This resistance becomes manifest the moment we try to place our attention on the source. It may seem like an effort to take the attention away from its habitual resting-place in this way, to take it away from the garage. However, the opposite is in fact the case. It is the cessation of focusing our attention on this sensation, this pseudo self in the body, which reveals the previously undetected efforts required to maintain it.

Meditation means to be open to the new at every moment. This is possible provided we don't fall asleep with the old, with the past, with an object. If the meditation is boring or repetitive, it means that we are in the garage. It is very simple to see. It is just a habit of remaining fixed on an object. Don't superimpose a limitation on your unlimited nature. Be the vastness knowingly.

In this meditation, we realign the way we feel with our understanding of the truth. If we understand that we are all pervading and limitless presence, why feel solid and limited? Don't stick to that which is solid and limited. Take off!

During the presence of any object, our presence is there. The object only indicates our presence. The object is not an obstacle. It is not necessary to fight the object, to try to get rid of it. Simply transcend the object by taking off from it into the presence in which it appears.

ය

When we die, does any trace of the individual remain?

Reality appears in accordance with our beliefs. If we feel that we are the body, then when the body dies, we die. If we think we are the mind and that the body and the world are subsets of the mind, then reality will appear according to this belief. In neither of these cases does the death of the body imply the end of the sense of separation.

When all these beliefs and images disappear through understanding, they disappear in consciousness, in us. However, we cannot convey through words the actual experience that we, as consciousness, do not die. All that can be conveyed through words is the understanding that there is no logical or experiential reason to believe that the consciousness which is seeing or understanding these words right this moment is personal. The moment we are open to the possibility that it is impersonal we are, by definition, open to the possibility that it does not die, because it is our experience that whatever dies is personal or limited. However, at this point it is only a logical inference. It is not an experience.

The actual experience that consciousness is not personal and that it does not die, however it comes to us, could be called enlightenment. It can be realized in many ways. It may be realized inside as knowingness, as direct evidence, or it may be realized through the world, when the world starts to appear in a miraculous way. The moment we are open to the possibility that the world is an appearance in consciousness, then the world loses its solidity. It even loses it dreamlike, magical quality. It goes beyond that. It becomes a revelation. It is both ordinary and extraordinary. If we look at it from the point of view of the person, of the individual, we see it as ordinary. If we look at it from the point of view of the impersonal "I," then we see the miracle. It doesn't matter how this experience comes about. What counts is the result.

Imagine you go on a safari with a guide. In this metaphor, the guide is the teacher. The guide knows where the tiger usually goes to drink in the evening, so he takes you there. The guide doesn't make the tiger appear. However, if you stay at that place, you are likely to see it.

Here we are taken to that place through the understanding that there is no evidence that consciousness is personal. At this point, we are open to the possibility that our consciousness, not some conceptual consciousness out in space somewhere totally apart from ourselves, but this very consciousness seeing these words right this moment, is God's consciousness. That is the one in you who hears, understands, feels, listens, sees. That is divine consciousness. It is not personal.

Once we are open to that possibility and stay in that openness, we are at the place where the tiger comes to drink. The tiger appears at its own pleasure. When we become very silent at that place, with no expectation of the tiger, that is when he chooses to appear. We have to be free from expectation. As long as there is expectation, we project our own tiger; we create our own image of the tiger.

The mind creates an image of God, of consciousness, and that is simply an agitation, a fabrication, a product of the mind and, ultimately, an avoidance of the real tiger. To understand that consciousness is divine implies that it lies beyond the personal mind. It implies that the mind cannot comprehend or apprehend it. The mind has to abdicate, to renounce any effort to know. Then something will happen, something out of the blue. Perhaps just a sound, something that comes fresh and reveals its origin. It is as though the silence becomes alive. It is like nothing becoming something and everything else becoming nothing.

When we stand at the edge of the river waiting for the tiger, it seems that the silence takes on a quality of its own. The mind comes to a stop. In the Indian tradition that is the moment when the teacher says, "You are that. You are that silence. You are that."

Don't expect anything, and you'll get everything.

6

There Is No Time, at All Times

During meditation I am aware of something localized in a particular place in the body. It is an experience of silence. It is where I would say, "I am."

An object is not silence, it appears in silence. An object by itself does not have the perfume of silence. It points towards silence when we are open to the now. Later on we discover that the object itself is permeated by silence. An object localized in the body is in a state of transition, but silence itself is not localized in the body.

Silence is that which remains after an experience has vanished, whether that experience is a thought, a feeling, a sensation, or a perception. It is silence, not the object that is experienced, which matters. It is always in the present, never in the past. In classical Greek the word *angel* meant "messenger." These "messages" are with us all the time. Whatever comes to us unexpected and unsolicited, for instance the singing of the birds or the coolness of the air, is in fact just such a message.

Listening implies welcoming our experience as it is, without subsequent thought, comment, judgment, interpretation, or analysis. It implies simply being open to these messages and allowing them to flow through us. The purpose of the message is to take us back to the one who has sent it. It is an invitation to the castle.

What is the difference between feelings and bodily sensations?

The word "feelings" has several meanings. For instance, confusion and depression are referred to as feelings, but both have a component in the mind. Both are felt as sensations in the body, but both are also based on the belief that we are separate persons.

In the case of confusion, the belief that we are separate entities triggers agitation of the mind whose purpose, in this case, is to protect the personal entity we believe ourselves to be, and to make it happy by ensuring that its desires are fulfilled. However, every time a desire is met, two or three new ones arise, so true fulfillment is not reached. Innumerable desires arise in this way, each looking for fulfillment in a different direction, until the situation is out of control. Confusion ensues when the thinking process spirals out of control, due to the multiplicity of the desires and fears of the ego and this in turn perpetuates the notion that we are separate entities.

It is also possible that we become caught in repetitive patterns of feelings in the body, which are more deeply rooted than our thoughts. In this case the mind may not be agitated, in fact, there might not be any thinking, but nevertheless, feeling continues.

For instance, we may feel that we are facing a dark, blank wall, and it requires a lot of courage to ask ourselves what this wall consists of. If we do this by completely welcoming the feeling, without any intention to reject it, we discover that it consists of layers of suppressed bodily sensations. These feelings are suppressed because, having labeled them "unpleasant," we are afraid or unwilling to experience them completely and they are therefore buried, so to speak, in the body.

If we completely welcome the feeling we may find that other feelings begin to surface, such as dullness, boredom, or lack, as if something were missing. If in turn we become interested in this lack and welcome it, other feelings such as fear or panic may start to rise. In this way layers of feelings are revealed, each with a location or locations in the body and as each in turn is welcomed, a new and deeper layer is revealed.

It may also happen during this process, that we have insights regarding the origin of a specific feeling, but it is not always the case. For instance, we may feel uncomfortable, and suddenly it becomes clear that it was as a result of finding a parking ticket on our windscreen that morning. The subsequent negative thoughts that were not processed on the spot create the ego at the level of the mind and leave a residue of subliminal feelings in our body, which in turn reinforce the sense of being a separate person.

One of the obstacles to processing our feelings is that they find hiding places in the body, thereby providing an opportunity for the ego, the sense of separation, to maintain itself. The body is a good hiding place for the ego because we are not fully aware of it. We live primarily in activities and thinking, and relatively little in feeling or perceiving. This lack of awareness at the bodily level means that we have little sensory knowledge of, for instance, our diaphragm or our face, and because we are unaware of them, they are ideal places for feelings such as fear to hide. It is for this reason that we include the body in our meditation.

It sounds as if these feelings have a realm of their own.

At the level of sensing we don't have a body as we usually conceive of it, we simply have the body as we actually sense it. However, it is left unexplored and largely unknown, because so many feelings are suppressed or unexpressed. A distinction is made between the body as we sense it and the body as we think of it, the body we perceive in the mirror. It is important to deal with the body as we actually sense it. We don't have to think about it and we don't have to worry about whether it is real or not. We are simply dealing with the actual sensations and feelings as they arise. Sometimes, we use words such as space, and describe these feelings as icebergs floating in the ocean and so on; these are just metaphors to help us do this exploration. They have no meaning per se.

These localizations in the body, where subliminal feelings lurk, are like dense clusters of energy. They are contracted areas that occupy our attention at the expense of other areas that are neglected. In this way a polarity is created between tension and dynamism on the one hand, and areas in the body of which we are not aware, on the other. If we give these neglected areas the attention they deserve, the two poles of the battery are put in contact, so to speak, and the tension is discharged. The system goes back to a state of balance and of stability.

The key is to listen to the bodily sensations. In the beginning we have to become aware that we are predominantly occupied with thinking and not enough with feeling the body. So we have to allow some time during the day for listening to bodily sensations without expecting anything, just seeing the body and allowing it to reveal itself as it is. Gradually, the body expands and at some point, either during the meditation or some time later, we realize that whereas we would previously have thought that we were in a room, for instance, we now feel that the room is actually in us. In fact, the body doesn't expand. Rather it has always been this expansion. It is just that the limitations that led us to believe the body was restricted vanish or are neutralized.

What is the essential difference between positive and negative emotions?

A negative feeling is a bodily sensation with an I-thought attached to it. It always has these two components. When we clearly understand that the "I" around which the feeling revolves is a fictitious entity then, as a result of this understanding, the I-thought is dropped. The feeling has now been downgraded to the rank of a bodily sensation. We now welcome this sensation; that is, we simply allow it to unfold in our benevolent and indifferent presence.

All sensations, like all thoughts, are dynamic. They are in motion. They move and change, some slowly, some fast. However, because they are dynamic they have a shelf life. They are no longer supported by the I-thought, by the thought, "He did this to me, so I am justified, et cetera." Being unsupported, they will evolve and change and eventually dissolve, although that is of no concern to us.

We have to be sure that there is no ulterior motive in our welcoming. If we secretly harbor the desire to get rid of an unpleasant sensation, then this desire itself will become another layer of resistance, of refusal, of contraction in the body.

Positive feelings are feelings that come directly from the source, unmediated through the thought or feeling of being a separate entity.

Sometimes I get a feeling of joy in my heart. It feels as though the heart doesn't have the capacity to hold it. Is there a connection between the joy and the silence?

Joy comes from silence. Silence expresses itself in many ways and joy is one of them. We cannot experience the silence as an object, but when we direct our heart towards silence, one of its responses is joy. It fills us up with joy. Our body is taken by joy. Sometimes, it is like an earthquake and we feel that the body is not able to take it. We may feel that the body is not able to resonate with this dimension and somehow that is true, but when we have these moments of grace, our body gives up some of its tension. The next time that we are taken by joy, it resonates a little better and opens up more until, after repeated exposure, it becomes a perfect instrument. If we touch a violin with our hand it cannot vibrate properly; we have to let go. In the same way our body has to be completely expanded to become a perfect instrument for joy.

Does consciousness or silence only express itself in beauty rather than in feelings like fear or anger? Aren't these things also an expression of silence and consciousness?

Yes, both the carrot and the stick take the donkey home. For example, imagine a fly landing on a painting by Rembrandt. It lands on a clear area of the painting and finds it beautiful. Then it walks a little and reaches a dark area and thinks it cold, dark, and fearful. So it takes off and only then does it see the whole painting. As long as it is looking at only the clear or the dark areas of the painting, the painting is not beautiful. These are opposing areas that, when put into perspective from a distance, contribute to the beauty and meaning of the whole painting.

It is true that everything, including fear and anger, is an expression of consciousness. However, in the case of negative feelings such as these, they are always founded on the thought or feeling of being limited and separate. We have to be careful of saying, "Well, everything is consciousness so anything goes and nothing matters." This is not implied in the statement, "Everything, including fear and anger, is an expression of consciousness."

We have to be very honest with ourselves. Is it really true of our own experience when we make this statement? Or are we just appropriating the Advaita teaching in order to avoid having to face our own fear and anger? It is easy to tell. Just ask yourself if there is any desire to get rid of these feelings. If the answer is, "Yes," then it shows that we do not deeply feel and understand that everything is an expression of consciousness.

If the answer is, "No, I have no desire to get rid of these feelings," then we have to ask ourselves why we did not completely accept the situation about which we became fearful or angry, in the first place. Surely that too was a perfect expression of consciousness and, while it may require an appropriate response, there would be no reason for fear or anger. However, if you understand and feel deeply that everything is an expression of consciousness, that's perfect. Live from that understanding and you will be a beacon.

However, if it is not our experience that everything is consciousness and if we have not come to the deep conclusion that it is so, then it means that some doubts and beliefs still remain. In this case, we have to investigate further.

If we do understand that it is true although it may not conform to our actual experience, then we can provisionally take the attitude that everything is consciousness; take it on trust. By trust, I do not mean belief. There is a big difference. By trust, I mean based on the understanding that there is nothing in our experience, nor is there any valid argument to suggest that there is anything that is not consciousness. If we have come to this conclusion we become truly open to the possibility that everything is consciousness. We put this conclusion to the test and we find that it is confirmed in our life. It is not a verbal, conceptual confirmation. It is a living confirmation. It is confirmed internally by causeless joy and peace, and it is confirmed externally by the unfolding revelation of the divine in the world.

೦෫

Sometimes, during meditation, thinking stops, the residual tension in the body is released, attention returns to the source, and nothing remains. However, my mind doesn't like this nothingness, so thinking starts again, and the process is repeated.

This nothingness is a blank state.

There is nobody in a blank state. It is not that I am experiencing nothingness; there is no thinking about nothingness. I couldn't tell you how long it had lasted.

Yes, but it lasted. Everything that lasts is in time. Everything that is in time is an object. Even if it is a blank object, it is still an object. What you were seeing was your expectation, a projection coming from expectation. It is still the mind.

81

When we go to understanding, it is totally free. We do not go there through effort but as a result of grace. When we try to solve a math problem, we don't make any effort because we don't know what to do. We just take a look at the data and then relax. In this effortless relaxation, the solution comes to us. In this timeless moment, we are in touch with the source of intelligence. Don't expect to see the timeless in time. Don't expect to make the timeless last. The timeless doesn't last. In our effort to see it in time, we make an object of it.

The situation was quite relaxed. In that blank, there doesn't seem to be anything one can do because there isn't any thinking. So one cannot say, "Here is a blank, therefore . . ."

You have created this blank and you have to wait until the energy that created it dissolves by itself. It is a manufactured state created by the desire to visualize the truth. You have to understand deeply that the truth cannot be visualized by the mind. It cannot be visualized in time, which is itself a product of mind.

Your energies and desires are focused on the truth, so all you have to do is understand clearly that truth is not an object. As a result all effort will stop. All your life, you have been accustomed to making efforts to attain goals, but now you have to let go of this residual effort. Once we have realized that all these goals cannot bring about happiness, there remains only one goal and that is to realize the Self.

When we understand that truth is not an object we realize simultaneously that we cannot be present as a person to enjoy it, because the object and the subject always come together. If truth cannot appear as an object, by the same token it cannot appear to a subject. The bad news is that the sense of being a person has to disappear. The good news is that the person never existed in the first place. When we have a moment of understanding we are free from the person, we are in our true nature. We cannot go there by our own effort. We go there in a moment of grace.

Can we be there knowingly?

We are there knowingly, but it is not an intellectual knowing. We can formulate it if needed. For instance, it is being formulated right now because a question has been asked. When we are happy, we are happy. When we notice intellectually that we are happy, we are no longer happy. In this case, we create a person who is happy. The truth is that we, as a person, are never happy because we *are* happiness itself.

So being there knowingly has nothing to do with the person. It is just a knowing.

Yes, it knows itself by itself. Joy knows itself. As children we didn't even know the word joy, we *were* joy. Later on we started to think about what joy meant, to make an object or a goal out of it, and therefore we lost it. Hence the search began. However, to be knowingly happy is to *be* happiness. To be knowingly intelligent is to *be* intelligence. This happiness, intelligence, and beauty is self-aware. It is not intellectually self-aware. It knows itself by itself. Shankara says in the Atmabodha, "It is self-luminous, unlike other objects that need the light of the sun or a lamp to be seen." This Self doesn't need any external light to be perceived. It is effortlessly self-aware.

In this moment you are effortlessly aware of my words and also of your own thoughts and reactions. You are that effortless space of awareness. Awareness is the most natural thing. It is the abode of happiness. It *is* happiness. However, we have forgotten that it is our treasure, that we already *are* it, and we think instead that happiness comes from external things. We don't need to make awareness self-conscious. It is already perfectly self-conscious.

Understand that what we most need and love is our own Self, and that it is not something far away out of reach. It is this very Self which, here and now, is aware of these words and whatever else you are experiencing in this moment. It is also the same Self that is experiencing everything that everybody else and every creature is experiencing in this moment.

Several teachers have said that the Self is only conscious of itself, and not of anything else.

It is true that it is only conscious of itself, but when that is fully understood it is also understood that everything is the Self, that nothing is apart from it. So whatever is experienced is experienced as the Self.

So consciousness doesn't see the birds, for instance, as something separate from itself. Birds are consciousness.

Ask yourself, "Can those birds which you are looking at now, be perceived without consciousness?" The answer is obviously, "No!" If the birds cannot be perceived without consciousness, how can we possibly claim that they are independent of consciousness? Try to separate the birds from consciousness. It is impossible!

It is only when we name our experience "the birds" that the thought apparently separates us from it. When there is perceiving, there is only perceiving. Nothing is perceived and nobody perceives. There is only the Self at every moment. There is only the Self and yet we think, "*I* perceived the *birds*." However, that is only a thought, and there is no thinker thinking this thought. In fact, there is no thought, there is just thinking. There is only the Self. There is only non-duality, at all times, and there is no time, at all times.

⊂3

I would like to ask about effort. The cat watching the mouse has to be vigilant, and sometimes that feels like effort.

As long as we think that there are mice to watch, there will be a cat, and we play cat and mouse. The moment we understand that the cat and mice are one, the game stops. As long as children play cops and robbers, they enjoy their game, but when they get tired, they have a break for candy. However, as long as we think that there is something to do, cat and mouse is a good game to play.

The same thing applies to self-inquiry. It is also a good game to play if we think that there is something to achieve. Ramana Maharshi was very clear on that point. He recommended self-inquiry for those who really wanted to do something. However, he would also say that there is nothing to be done. "Just enjoy yourself. Abide in the Self. You are that already," he would say. Most people didn't listen, so they would play cat and mouse.

At the beginning of the weekend I experienced a spontaneous openness. Then there were layers of repressed energy, in the form of dryness, the same blank wall. At these times the natural openness is not perceived. Could you speak more of the patience required in the exploration of this depression, this dullness, this dislike?

We should love our dislike, because even our dislike is the Self. Love is a prerequisite for understanding, dissolution, and freedom. As long as we maintain a separation between ourselves and our dislikes, we perpetuate it. As long as we maintain a conflict with our enemy, we perpetuate the hostility. The moment we embrace our enemy, he lays down his arms. We have to stop separating ourselves from our dislikes, to stop saying, "I don't like my dislikes."

I've experienced love coming into my dislikes, but it takes patience and courage.

It is not a manufactured love. On the progressive path we could practice permeating our dislikes with love but that would be a manufactured love, a superimposition of one feeling on top of another. I am not saying that this type of approach could not be beneficial, but it is not what is being spoken about here.

Love means to be open, simply to include whatever arises within consciousness without preference, interference, or intention, not to manufacture anything, but to see the facts as they are. See your dislike about the fact, which is itself simply another fact, and see your dislike about your dislike, which is yet another fact. We have piled up feelings, one on top of another, and we have to start dismantling them from the top of the pile. The top of the pile is always in the now. It is whatever is presenting itself in this moment. However, there is nothing to do about the pile. It dismantles itself in our benevolent, welcoming presence.

Love is all-inclusive. Some people only love their own children. When some women have their first child, they love it so much that there is no love left for their partner. This is a case of love being applied only to one realm but not to the whole. The Self is intelligence, beauty, and love. Since everything is the Self, we should apply intelligence, beauty, and love to everything and see everything as intelligence, beauty, and love.

I feel that this applies to everything, whether it is the birdsong or the sound of the heater. If I am distracted by thoughts, I am not receptive. But when I am simply receptive, the "I" disappears, and there is space for everything.

There can be thinking without the sense of being a person. What you have just expressed is a good example of that. We should not limit the realm of our experience to perceiving and sensing; that would be limiting God. We should include thinking. However, at some point, the thinking that is based on a personal entity drops away by itself.

I don't think there is anything I can do about thinking, but I can choose silence when it comes. Is that thinking again?

Know that ultimately everything is silence.

It is difficult to see everything as silence if we divide things into beautiful and ugly. Out of love for the truth, there is a tendency to choose the beautiful in preference to the ugly. However, whatever one is disgusted with or hates tends to come back with quite a force. Can you comment on this?

When we love our hate, we stop hating. Love always wins. To love hatred means to welcome it. It doesn't mean that we should do what it tells us to do, but we shouldn't suppress it either. When we love hatred we put ourselves out of the process of hatred, and love begins.

But it is so strong. Where does it come from?

It is the old habit of thinking that we are separate. Just let it go. Go back to the child in yourself. Be kind to it and listen to it, because the child is the Self. The child doesn't hate or love; it just is. Don't resist it. Just surrender. What is important is to get rid of the notion that there is something to change, something to fix, that things are not the way they should be. Stop playing God. When we stop playing God, we are God.

I would like to ask about pain and suffering.

There is a distinction. Do you mean pain or suffering?

I think it is artificial to say that there is a difference. In many cases I would say they go hand-in-hand.

Suffering, psychological suffering, is not necessary and can be avoided. However, there is certainly pain and that cannot be avoided. Hence the distinction. To enjoy pleasure and suffer pain is part of the package of having a body. Psychological suffering is the most intense of all and it is not necessary. If you don't want to make a distinction, I cannot explain why psychological suffering is not necessary.

Psychological suffering is related to the notion of a sufferer, a person. It is always related to past and future. Consider for instance the case of my friend William Samuel. During World War II he was in China. He was assigned a Chinese interpreter who was a Taoist sage, although he didn't know it at the time. The first thing that he noticed about this man was that he was always happy, smiling and enjoying.

One day they were in great danger. William's platoon was being pursued by the Japanese who were very close. They were running back towards their lines. There were hills on the horizon and the sage pointed to the purple line of the mountains and said to William, "Look, how beautiful!" William said, "It was the last thing I would have thought about at that moment."

Some time later William discovered that three months earlier the sage's wife had been raped and killed by the Japanese and that they had also killed his two sons. That's what triggered his interest in this man, and he eventually became his student. This Taoist sage was free from the past. He may have been in pain, but he was not suffering on account of the death of his wife and children. In seeing the beauty of the purple hills while under enemy fire, he was teaching a wonderful lesson in courage and love. It is hard to imagine more atrocious circumstances.

Not too many people are in a position of such psychological and spiritual maturity. Look at the millions of people that you see on television.

Of course, but we are here to discuss another possibility. We are not here to save the world or alleviate the suffering in the world. We first have to save ourselves from suffering, because unless we are free from suffering, we cannot help others. As long as we see this world as a world of misery, we perpetuate the misery. It is only in the moment that we see the beauty of the whole painting and not just the light places, that we are able to convey this sense of beauty, this sense of eternity, to others.

All suffering is based on the notion that death is bad. Whether we are aware of it or not, suffering is about the fear of death. People are willing to suffer a great deal of physical pain rather than die. The belief that we are subject to death is the cause of suffering and this suffering prevents us from truly living, because instead we live a life based on this false belief. This belief projects us into the past and future. It is incompatible with happiness. Understand that there is no death.

Some people experience tremendous mental suffering and commit suicide to end the suffering. You say that suffering has its roots in the fear of death, but they are saying that death is preferable to suffering, so how is the fear of death the cause of suffering in these cases?

These people have mistaken the origin of their suffering. They want to escape a situation that is unbearable, but psychological suffering is always created by the person. It hinges around the sense of being separate. Nobody imposes this on us. I am not saying that suicide is always wrong. There are circumstances in which it may be the only way out.

Many people say that they aren't frightened of dying but rather the suffering that leads up to it.

Yes, but the origin of this suffering is the notion of being a person, a separate individual. This separate individual is subject to fear. It is this fear that generates suffering.

How can we be free of the fear of death?

We are afraid of death and focus our minds on it. We are hypnotized by our fear of it. However, the true question is about life, not death. Before we understand who dies, we need to understand who lives. It is too soon to understand death, but we can understand life. Life is present right now. So, who is alive? When we find out what life is, we may also discover that there is no death. After all, who is there to die?

This path is a path of joy, not fear. We see the world according to our own projections. If we believe we are separate individuals, we will be subject to desire and fear, and we will suffer. A suffering world will then appear in accordance with this belief and we will perpetuate it, without realizing that we are actually creating it. If we see a world of injustice, we become injustice and perpetuate it.

The implication of this may be disappointing, but it is the only way out of suffering for ourselves and for others. Unless we are free from suffering, how can we help someone else?

89

For instance, consider the case that you believe that death exists and that it is the ultimate evil. You have a friend dying of cancer in the hospital. You visit him and ask him how he is and tell him not to worry. He knows he is dying and that everyone is lying to him. You are his best friend and you come and lie to him also, not perhaps by telling him that everything will be fine, you may be more honest than that, but you will still be piling up your own fear on top of his.

It would be a different situation if you were free from the fear of death. You would just go and listen. Whatever is going to happen will happen. Whatever you say, which will of course be unpredictable, will somehow work miracles. You do the best you can, given the circumstances.

If we think that death is the ultimate evil, something we have to fight against, we fail to understand that fighting is simply more suffering. We will see our mission as a war. War against poverty, war against social injustice, war against death, war against illness, but nevertheless still war. War is the perpetuation of suffering.

It is very different if we see that things are not that important. This life is a dream and we play our part in it. If we are detached, we play our part as well as we can and because of our detachment, we play our best. We are like a violinist who doesn't worry about the critics while performing, and is therefore going to play well. It is the same thing here. We are not attached to the results because there are no results. It is a game and there are no positive or negative outcomes. This attitude will enable us to give the highest form of help we are capable of.

We are talking about death of the apparent individual. Of course, there is physical death, the death of the body. A world without death would have no beauty, no yellow leaves in the autumn. It would be boring. There would be no change because change implies death. A world without death would be a frozen world. The fact is that we want to make the world better than God does.

90

When we see a young person dying and everyone is crying, we wonder, "Why is this necessary? What function does it have?" The sun has a function. We understand a lot of things as a function, but what is the function of an occurrence such as the death of a young person?

We cannot judge from the outside. We can only see from the inside. See that all events in our life, the happy ones and especially the unhappy ones, have made us grow in beauty, understanding, wisdom, and love.

So these times offer the possibility for growth?

Yes. I have a friend who is very ill and is dying of lung cancer. She told me that she gives thanks for what has happened to her, because without it she would never have been interested in life and would never have experienced and known what she knows now. She does not want things to be different. Her teacher, Robert Adams, used to say, "All is well and everything is unfolding just as it should."

We want to play God, to tell God what to do and how to make the perfect universe. We would like no mosquitoes, no death, no flu, no cancer, no autumn, no seasons, and no bugs. We want everything in the right place. By thinking in this way, we are forgetting the perfection that is evident from moment to moment. We are living in the past, in the future, in thinking. The now is always free from suffering, problems, and separation. It is always free from ego. In the now there is no ego. The ego cannot live in the now.

If we think there is a problem with the world, we have a problem! We are not the problem, we are freedom. The world appears in accordance with our views. It is for this reason that keeping our mind on the problem only perpetuates it. You have to de-hypnotize yourself from the problem, which is the object, and to turn towards the Self. The Self will deal with the problem in an appropriate way. Surrender to the Self.

Don't allow yourself to think in terms of problems. Think in terms of solutions if you want, or in terms of the universal solution, which is the Self. Solution means to dissolve. Everything gets dissolved in the Self. You didn't come here to have your ideas about suffering reinforced. You came here to hear a different tune, a shocking tune!

Sometimes I feel that this impersonal approach is cold and distant.

The opposite is in fact the case. "Impersonal" means not based on the thought or feeling of being a separate entity. When we are free from this belief and feeling, we are compassion itself. "Compassion" means to "feel with" or to "empathize." When our experience of a so-called other is not filtered through thoughts or feelings of separation, we are simply present as this openness, this pure sensitivity, this impartial, loving, benevolent space. As a result of this, we empathize with the so-called other. We do not project our own interpretations, our beliefs, our fears onto them. As a result of this our response is appropriate and effective, even if it may not appear to be so to begin with.

True intimacy is only possible when thoughts and feelings of separation are not present. That is what intimacy is, the absence of separation. We are never intimate as persons. That is why so many relationships go wrong. We want to be intimate as separate entities. It is not possible. The person is the refusal of intimacy. In the absence of the person, we are intimacy itself. Intimacy with animals, people, the universe, everything.

You say that there is no death, but I can't see how one could possibly know whether there is or is not. In the now there is the now and we know what happens there.

In your idea of the now there is a future, but in reality there is no future, change, or death in the now. The now is not the opposite of the future or the past. It contains past, present, and future. The future in this present moment is a concept. If you believe that this concept is actually true, you are being eaten by time. Show me the future!

If we take a close look at the body as we actually experience it in this moment, we realize that it is simply made of changing sensations. It is very different from the body we conceptualize or from the one we see in the mirror. Each time a sensation vanishes, the body as we actually experience it vanishes too. The body dies at every moment.

In fact everything vanishes from moment to moment, except the consciousness in which it appears. By associating consciousness with the body we make it an object in time. The consciousness that is in time is not true consciousness. The consciousness understanding these words right now is beyond time. It is changeless and timeless. Everything else, the body, the mind, and the world, is changing all the time, coming and going. Consciousness is the antecedent of the body, the mind, and the world. Hence Jesus' saying, "Before Abraham was, I am." There is no goal, motion, or change in consciousness.

That which comes and goes is not you. It comes and goes in you. How often have you said, "*I* come, *I* go, *I* will die?" But you don't know what "I" means. You have to find out who you are, what this "I" is, which means what this consciousness is. Then you can ask the question, "Do 'I,' this consciousness, die?"

Logical reasoning cannot answer this question one way or the other. When we say, "I die," we imply that we already have the answer. However, if we inquire about our actual experience, we discover that we cannot answer the question, because the mind has no access to consciousness.

Having discovered this, we find ourselves genuinely open to the possibility that consciousness is not tied to the body, because the body obviously dies. Without this openness, fear will prevent us from looking in the right direction. We will not have the courage or the will to move on. It is from beyond fear that we receive the answer. It is beyond the ego.

At times when the path is clear one reaches for something to depend on, but it is clear that any technique is simply going to take one into the past by virtue of its being a technique.

That is good because there is no path.

But there seems to be a process in time.

A path implies someone to travel on it. Find out who wants to travel and it will take you to the end of the path, to the pathless path.

Is desire a hindrance and should certain objects be avoided?

This is not a path of detachment from objects, of depriving oneself of life. On the contrary, life should be a celebration. We need to discover what life is before we can truly celebrate it. When we find out what life really is, a natural detachment takes place. This detachment is effortless, because our discovery gives us such absolute happiness, cures us so radically of fear, gives us such an ease of being and freedom, that the usual objects of desire seem pale in comparison. In other words, we are not detaching ourselves from objects through practices or disciplines; they are detaching themselves from us as a result of understanding and causeless joy. The objects are all still available but the difference is that we no longer use them to obtain happiness. We use them to celebrate happiness.

There are no regrets on this path. We can still do whatever we previously wanted to do but we do it in freedom, because we understand everything we do as a celebration of our freedom, not as a means of fulfillment. When we have this understanding and attitude towards life, the universe cooperates with us. It becomes our accomplice.

There is a Sufi story of the prophet Mohammed who, before he fell in love with God, had the desire to be a great speaker. However, he fell in love with God and became a truth seeker and then a truth lover, and he forgot about his desire. It left him. One day, God appeared in a dream and said, "Mohammed, I am going to give you the talent of speech." Mohammed replied, "But I don't have that

94

desire any longer. Now I am in love with you, so I no longer care for such things." However, God said, "Nevertheless, you once had this desire and I am going to make you such a famous speaker that your name will be sung five times a day in all the minarets on the surface of the earth."

The universe has no choice but to appear as true. We cannot only grow in confidence and certainty on the inside, although we may have tremendous inner experience. If this was the case we may wonder, after a few days or years, whether or not we dreamt it or made it up. We also need the universe to confirm that what we know on the inside is fully consistent in all realms of our outer experience. Therefore, it is very important to implement what we have understood; otherwise it remains frozen. We need to take it out of the freezer, put it in the microwave, and eat it!

How can we be free of sensations or feelings?

A mirror is not stained or damaged by the images it reflects within itself. In the same way, consciousness is not hurt by, and is completely free from the images, fears, perceptions, thoughts, and sensations that appear in it. Therefore, as you are already free from all these sensations and feelings, and always have been, why do you want to practice in order to become free?

They sometimes leave some agitation.

Only the memory of them does.

However, simply the memory of the truth of the consciousness may not have the power to remove the agitation.

Your question implies a desire to get rid of the agitation, a dislike of the agitation. By disliking it, you move away from the mirror. You no longer understand that you are the mirror and that the mirror can never be hurt, touched, or put into motion by the agitation. If the agitation bothers us, it means that we have mistakenly identified with something in the mirror instead of with the mirror itself. We should take our stance as the mirror again, which we always are anyway.

The mirror doesn't care about the agitation. It is unconcerned whether the images reflected in it are static, slowly evolving, or hectic. From the vantage point of the mirror, it is all the same. However, if we return to being the mirror, the images themselves will slow down.

In this celebration of life, it is a relief that one doesn't have to exorcise the ghosts of insecurity and all those things, that we don't have to dig them out of the cupboard and get rid of them.

Yes, digging them up doesn't get rid of them. It perpetuates them. The one who wants to dig them up and get rid of them is the same one that is at the root of insecurity. The ego can never get rid of the ego. Just find out who feels insecure.

Does one just leave all that alone, without addressing it?

Don't go back to your fear if fear is not coming to you; that would be masochistic. Don't worry about anything. It is not even necessary to think in spiritual terms. When we are happy and free from problems, we are in our true spiritual state, the perfect state. That is what God wants us to be and at these times we are fulfilling God's desire. It is only when we think that things need to be changed that we start getting into trouble.

There is the idea that you have to look at all that.

Let ghosts sleep, don't wake them up. Celebrate and just get used to celebrating more and more.

7

God Is Very Mischievous

I have a sense of returning to the fundamental consciousness that everyone has. Is it a recognition rather than a process?

There is nobody to return and nowhere to return to. All bodies are in this "nobody." The entire "where" is in this "nowhere."

But is it a recognition?

In the Advaita tradition, the example of a necklace is often used. A woman is looking for a necklace everywhere, only to find at the end of the search, that it was always around her neck. While she is looking, she thinks, "I have lost my necklace," and when she finds it, "I have found it again." The question is whether she had really lost it. She only thought that she had lost it.

What is the role of the teacher?

The teacher does not give you a new necklace but just asks you to look in the mirror. The teacher does not give you anything new. One should be careful about any misunderstanding in this respect. Indian society is very hierarchical, highly differentiated and, due to these social traditions that have nothing to do with the truth, the guru is way above the fray. For instance, the Brahmin caste is above everybody else and this is an impediment at some point. Although Ramana Maharshi was a Brahmin, he would eat with everybody else at his ashram. There was a special dining room for the newcomers who were Brahmins and initially they would eat there. However, since the teacher was not there, they would eventually move in with everybody else. He was always very careful not to be put on a pedestal. He would even become angry if he received special treatment and rightfully so, because he didn't see himself as different from anyone else.

One has to be careful about traditions that make a god of the teacher. It is true that the teacher is speaking the truth, but from his or her vantage point, everything is speaking the truth. For instance, when the student is asking a question, it is truth speaking to the teacher. Usually, when the teacher dies, when his body dies, his pedestal is raised up to the ceiling at least. Then, each subsequent year, it rises a couple more meters, and so eventually it is at an almost infinite distance from us! We forget that the teacher was and is what we are.

A teacher is very human as a person, very much like us. There is a beautiful poem by Thayumamavar, a sixteenth century Indian poet, in which he compares the teacher with a deer who is sent towards a herd of deer, in order to lure them towards the hunter. God is the hunter in this metaphor and the teacher is the deer that is sent to the herd. There has to be a real deer or the herd would feel that there was a trap and would not follow.

There should not be any difference between the teacher and the student. It is natural that there is respect because the teacher sees the Self in you. Respect calls for respect. Love calls for love. At the same time, the teacher should make realization seem easy. If a teacher makes it seem difficult and out of reach, then find another one!

The teacher that takes us to freedom, known in India as the Satguru or the Karana guru, wants our freedom above all else. In the Karana guru's presence, we feel this total freedom with respect to the rules. Deep inside we know that there are no rules, although it may be appropriate to follow the rules if a situation requires it. There is this total freedom. The teacher doesn't judge you. Everything is OK. You are OK.

Take Robert Adams, for instance. He was a beautiful loose cannon! He was an expression of this freedom. It was this quality that enabled you to be free from your own conditioning, from what you thought you ought or ought not to do.

Freedom is the highest good. It is that which is closest to the Self. Above love, above intelligence, above beauty, there is freedom. That is why this game we are playing is called the game of bondage and liberation.

Although I appreciate what you have just said, the conditioning is deeply rooted. I am not sure whether I am doing things the right way or not, and I feel that I could, in freedom, make some big mistakes.

In freedom there is no right and no wrong. There are no mistakes because there is nobody to make mistakes. If we are afraid of making a mistake when we do something, the most important thing is to take a closer look at the original intention. If our original intention is pure, that is, if it is motivated by our interest in, and our love for the truth, for freedom, we may make a mistake but it will not matter. Life will take care of us.

For instance, imagine a student who goes to a teacher out of love for the truth and, although he is unaware of it, the teacher is not genuine. In this situation the student will compel the teacher to speak the truth because of the sincerity of his intention. Nothing is lost. The student, who had obviously gone to the wrong place to find the truth, will still receive the correct guidance at that moment. Of course, later on the teacher will be dropped. What happens to the teacher is a different story.

Would you say that at that point the student needed that teacher?

Everything that happens to us teaches us. Everything is our teacher. The beautiful friends that we have known and who have helped us on the path and the plank that hit us on the head were both our teacher.

When having to make decisions in terms of other people's freedom, for example one's children, there is very often a concern that what is happening is right. It is not always clear where the freedom lies for the person you're looking after.

It is not for us to decide what his or her freedom is. All we have to know is our own freedom. Once we know our own freedom, this freedom will express itself spontaneously in whatever we do and say. When the child hears and sees this, it will resonate with its own freedom and it will subsequently discover what its own freedom is. To make people free, all you have to do is to be free. It is our freedom that makes them free, not our desire to make them free. The desire to make them free binds them. In this freedom, we don't know what is going to happen.

How do you achieve freedom?

We are freedom. We cannot achieve it. Whatever is achieved can also be lost. That which we are, is free from everything. To begin with we discover the freedom that could be called "freedom from," just as the mirror is free from the objects that are reflected in it. We discover that we are the mirror. Later on, instead of being like a mirror, in which everything appears to be reflected from outside, we become more like a television in which everything that appears on the screen is the creation of the television. Then we are not only free "from," but also free "to," free to create. Everything that comes out of this freedom is our own creation. It is not something external.

If I imagine that I am free just as I am, with my ego as it is, is this freedom?

See what you call "my ego." This is the first step towards freedom and the last one. You say "my ego." How do you know you have an ego?

I am aware of separateness.

So what is the ego? Is it the separateness or that which is aware of it? The ego is the separateness and that which is aware of this separateness is not ego, it is the Self, and that is free. The moment it

100

is clear that the ego is not what we are, but that it is something perceived in the mirror, we realize that we do not need to make the mirror free.

I always seem to feel separate one way or another.

Is the separateness always present, for instance when you hear or see something? No! The separateness is perceived. It is present only as long as it is perceived. Irrespective of what the separateness is made of, whether it is beliefs, thoughts, or bodily sensations, where is it when something else is present, for instance when you are reading a book or watching television? It is not perceived. Understand that there are many moments, for instance right now, when separateness is not perceived.

I hear what you are saying but I find it difficult to take on board.

You don't have to take it on board. Who is there to take it on board or not? We don't have to say, "Yes" or "No" to the truth, because truth is truth. For instance, even in relative truth, the sun rises every morning, whether we say, "Yes" or "No" to this fact. The truth is independent of whatever we think about it or whatever we tell it to be.

When you are looking at a landscape, thinking, watching television, reading a book, and so on, there's no separation. Perhaps it comes and goes but when you are really experiencing whatever it is, when you are listening to these words for instance, there is no separation. Is consciousness present during these moments? Of course! So you well know moments during which consciousness is not tied to the sense of separation, to the ego. The ego comes and goes.

You have understood this intellectually, but it is more than intellectual. It is your actual experience that, like the images in the mirror, the ego comes and goes, because it is a perceived object made of a thought or a feeling. All that needs to be done is to remain as awareness. This awareness is freedom. Understand that you are this freedom in which everything is allowed to come into existence.

When one is lost in a book or in the television, it doesn't seem to be very satisfying; it's not enough somehow.

I am not encouraging you to get lost in books or television. I used the example to show that although consciousness is always present, the feeling that we are separate is not. In this way we understand that consciousness is independent of the ego. This is very important. We can dissociate the ego from awareness.

If you are not happy reading books, don't read them. If you are not happy doing anything, don't do it. Nobody forces you. This "follow your bliss" attitude will lead you towards bliss. Read the book as long as it makes you happy. When the book no longer makes you happy, put it aside. Don't keep reading out of habit. Happiness is the highest good. It is sacred.

The problem is not the first time we have happiness. The problem is when we try to repeat it, when we try to reproduce it. We shouldn't repeat things. The first time is fine but not the second!

A friend of mine told me that he had a hundred LSD experiences. During the first he had a wonderful mystical experience. The following ninety-nine experiences were a waste of time and energy. Follow your bliss. Follow your happiness, knowing that happiness is always the place of the heart, the place of God. However, God is very mischievous and keeps changing the place where it appears! We can never predict where it will appear next and this keeps us open and awake. All we can do is be ready for any appearance. Being ready for God to appear anywhere and in any form is called, "Abiding in the Self, abiding in the source."

You say we should abide in the Self, in the source, for God to appear. Are God and Self the same?

Of course they are the same. That which appears in the source is the source. God is everything.

❧

Krishnamurti said that if one human being realized his true nature, then it would have an impact on the whole human consciousness. How could one human being influence consciousness?

When we understand that we are not a personal entity, we stop reacting to aggression or unlovingness. We welcome it and let it dissolve within us. We are like a black hole. Such a black hole is very efficient. We need them in society. They gradually influence their surroundings. Whenever we welcome, at the same time we radiate love. We may not be aware of it in the beginning, but this is exactly what happens. When we are in welcoming, we are radiant with love, and love has this transforming power. Therefore, be a black hole.

If you think you are somewhere, there must be someone there. Don't think of yourself as realized or non-realized. Just be this black hole. Understand this benevolent welcoming as your own true nature. Then the appearance or disappearance of old belief systems will be no more than a cloud crossing the blue sky. Don't worry about the clouds. It is a kind of perfectionism and Puritanism that wants us to be perfect as a person. Forget it! The body is not perfect; it is going to die. The mind is not perfect. It does not always make the right decisions. Don't try to be what you cannot be. Just be what you already are. You are perfection already, so don't try to be perfect with the body. Be what you are, which is perfection. Then see that everything, including your own mistakes, is an emanation from perfection.

I'm not telling you to be arrogant about your mistakes by saying, "God does it all." You may think so, but still apologize to the other person if appropriate, even though you realize that nobody did it, nobody as a person, that is. Be loving towards those who have not always been right, because you also have not always been right. Understand that so-called teachers are also human beings. Allow them the freedom to make mistakes. Allow yourself the freedom to make mistakes.

One of the greatest sages in history, the Sixth Patriarch of China, Hui Neng, was once asked, "Can you see your Buddha nature?" This was a code for, "Are you enlightened?" He didn't say, "Yes" or "No" but rather, "All I can see are my own mistakes." By answering in that way, he was first of all teaching the student that our true nature cannot be seen. He was also showing true humility by acknowledging that as a human being he was not above the fray. By acknowledging his own mistakes and by his humility, he was transcending.

If we expect a human being to be perfect, it means we are expecting ourselves to be perfect. We are looking for the impossible. It means we are missing the mark and we somehow know it deep inside. We cannot make imperfection perfect. We cannot change what is limited and make it limitless. That which is limitless has always been limitless. That which is perfect has always been perfect. See that we are that, not the limited body-mind. That is the path to perfection. Beware of teachers who tell you, "I am perfect as a human being." They are challenging you, so put them to the test.

Ramana Maharshi was always very patient and gentle, although he could be firm. Nisargadatta Maharaj was always losing his temper and was very impatient. If it is true that both were realized beings and that once you've realized your true nature you are quite indifferent to outside events, how are we to understand this loss of temper in Nisargadatta?

Even before his self-realization, Ramana Maharshi was a very gentle being. The story goes that his peers would beat him up and he wouldn't respond. However, I have heard that sometimes he would get angry and throw apples at people, even after his realization.

But Nisargadatta Maharaj is the one that interests me. Is it as if one light is filtering through body-minds which have different colors, and that the purer the body-mind, the more light it lets through?

This kind of explanation is an attempt to formulate something that cannot be put into words. They may be helpful for a certain person at a certain time but ultimately we have to go beyond all concepts.

There are many ways of expressing one's feelings. Everything is ultimately the truth. Those who have realized the truth become beacons, and some are more powerful than others. Some sages find that their perceptions are not harmonized so they don't have a feeling for beauty. Others find their minds are not harmonized, so

104

they don't have clarity. For others, their feelings are not harmonized so they don't radiate love. It doesn't mean they are not sages. They all radiate all of these qualities to a certain extent, but it is manifested in different ways depending on how far this understanding has permeated the mind, the body, and the world.

The important thing is to implement this understanding of consciousness in all realms of our life, to transpose what we have understood at the intellectual level to the level of feeling and sensing, so that everything becomes integrated in our life. When this occurs our feeling, sensing, and thinking will be harmonized with the source.

Both Ramana Maharshi and Nisargadatta have gone and there is no division in that which remains. There is only one Self and only one sage. As long as we think of ourselves as separate people, we will see a separate person in the teacher or the sage. That is not the experience of the sage. The sage experiences himself or herself as consciousness and there is only one consciousness. It seems mysterious, but it gets clarified the moment we understand that we are all one single consciousness that expresses itself in an incredible, extraordinary diversity from moment to moment.

If one believes that other people are part of consciousness, do we not have a duty to be compassionate towards other people and to try to make the world a better place to live in?

If it were your experience that there is only one consciousness, this question wouldn't arise. You say, "If one believes that other people are part of consciousness . . ." We are not *part of* consciousness, we *are* consciousness, the *same* consciousness. We all have this invisible witness in common and it is this witness that we call "I." It is not your private witness.

This has to be clearly understood. To begin with, take it as a possibility. Compassion comes at a later stage. Compassion is a natural consequence of understanding who we are. We cannot be compassionate without first finding out who we are. Until such a time, don't try to be compassionate. Be compassionate towards yourself by finding out who you are. That is true compassion and it is also the most efficient compassion. It is the fastest way to help the world. If we do not know who we are, our actions will come from ignorance and they will only add to ignorance. When we know who we are, we realize that the world doesn't need to be saved. First find your true nature and then see whether there is still a world that needs saving. When we find out who we are, the world as we normally conceive of it disappears, for it is no longer experienced as being separate or outside of ourselves.

Ramana Maharshi says the mind receives reflected light from consciousness and this seems to accord with the Platonic analogy of the cave. However, the Ashtavakra Gita suggests forgetting this question of reflected consciousness. I respect the Ashtavakra Gita and Ramana Maharshi, but am confused about these two perspectives.

In these images, consciousness is the source of light. Like the sun it is self-luminous and autonomous. It generates its own light. However, although the moon resembles the sun and seems to illuminate objects, it is not in fact self-luminous. It derives its luminosity from the sun. In the same way the mind derives its cognitive power, its faculty of knowing, from the source, from consciousness. In this analogy luminosity stands for consciousness. In the same way that the sun shines with its own light and needs no other source of light to be seen, so consciousness knows itself by itself.

To say that the mind, which is represented by the moon, is not self-luminous, means that it is not conscious by itself. It is seen but it cannot see. The mind appears to have consciousness of its own and to know things, just as the moon appears to have its own light and to illuminate objects.

However, the moon is illumined by the sun, in the same way that the mind, thoughts, are illumined by consciousness. Consciousness is the perceiver. The moon seems to illumine objects on earth during the night, but it doesn't illumine them by its own light. It is sunlight, reflected by the moon, which illumines these objects. The moon is in fact an object that, like all other objects, is itself illumined by the sun. It is in fact consciousness and consciousness alone that enables objects to be known.

In order to clarify this further, Ramana Maharshi also used an ancient Advaitic tool apart from self-inquiry and other skillful means, which was to distinguish between the perceiver and the perceived. He would clearly say that the Self is the perceiver and that everything else, including the ego, is perceived. He also said that it is enough for the truth seeker to understand this distinction, in order to get back to perceiving. Only consciousness, the Self, truly has the perceiving power. The mind only seems to have it, just like the moon.

What do you make of the notion of avatars?

Everything is an avatar.

There is a notion that certain beings . . .

This notion is also an avatar. Everything that is manifested is the Self manifesting itself. These ideas about avatars are concepts. It is better to understand that everything is the Self, because that abolishes all distinctions. It takes us directly to the truth. Everything is God, so everything is an avatar of God. Everything is the Son of God. Everything that appears is the Self coming out of the void.

But you just made a distinction between the perceiver and the perceived.

Yes, that was for a different question! That question was a theoretical one about how to see that two sides of the same truth are in fact one, in order to understand that there is no inconsistency between the teachings of the Ashtavakra Gita and the teachings of Ramana Maharshi.

When we say that we are the perceiver and not the perceived, it is in order to go to the experience of pure consciousness, of Turiya. Usually, we believe that we are the body-mind, so the truth seeker has to be reminded that the body-mind is perceived. That which perceives is "I," consciousness. Everything that is perceived is an object.

107

It is necessary to make this distinction because we usually identify with an object, a fragment. We don't think, "I am the table, I am my clothes, I am my car." However we do think, "I am this body and the rest is not me." We identify with a fragment of our experience. In order to remove this identification, the Advaita tradition uses a two-step process. In the first step it says, "You are not that which is perceived, you are the perceiver." In this step we reject everything that is perceived as not being ourselves. We reject the table, the car, the clothes, the body, and the mind, and this leads us to the experience of pure consciousness. Then, as the universe of names and shapes reappears, it is understood to reappear in the light of consciousness, out of consciousness, as a projection of consciousness. Therefore, the second step is, "Everything is consciousness. Consciousness is the source and substance of everything." It is not like the sun that seems to illumine things that are already there, but rather that without consciousness they simply don't exist, nothing exists, so they are nothing other than consciousness. Everything is consciousness. The metaphor of the ocean is more appropriate in this case. All objects are like waves that arise out of this ocean, are made of the same substance as the ocean, and dissolve back into it. Therefore, they are always one with it.

In the first step, only "I" is consciousness and the rest is perceived. This step is an effective way of loosening our identification with objects, including the body and the mind. However, when objects reappear, some duality will still remain between "I" as consciousness and that which appears. Having discovered "I," a second step is therefore necessary in which everything that appears is understood and experienced to be consciousness, "I."

It is important to understand this because sometimes, when we are only referring to the first stage, it might appear that credibility is being given to the idea of the existence of a subject and an object. This is not the case. It is simply that, at that moment, we are only talking about one part of the process. This first part of the process does not represent a complete understanding of the true nature of our experience, and yet for most people it is a necessary staging post.

Sometimes I experience ecstatic or very peaceful states, but they do not last, and the rest of my life seems bland and uninteresting by comparison.

You feel that things need to be changed. You feel that things are not satisfactory as they are, that they are not unfolding as they should. Don't worry about things. Although these states, these samadhis, have a mystical quality to them, they are objective experiences. They are very refined objects, but nevertheless they are still objects. They are traps. Just as, on the path of knowledge, powers or siddhis are at some point a trap, so also are samadhis. Siddhis are the active part of the trap and samadhis are the passive part. Samadhis are the last layer of ignorance, anandamayakosha, the layer of the illusion of bliss. If we are attached to bliss, we kill bliss. As William Blake said, "He who binds himself to a joy does the winged life destroy."

I had an experience thirty years ago in which I was blissfully happy, everything was so vibrant, but it vanished and I have never experienced it again.

It takes time to understand that the happiness in a happy state never comes and goes. Whatever was happy in that happy state thirty years ago, is still present right now. It is happiness itself. You objectified it and attached it to an experience that happened thirty years ago. To be hypnotized by the past prevents us from being knowingly this happiness in the present. Understand that the perfume of this experience is still present. It has never left you. In fact it is precisely because it has never left you, that you keep thinking about it.

I have had other experiences in which everything is not vibrantly happy but peacefully happy, and everything just flows. There is no feeling of restlessness or ego. I was just referring to that particular one because it was so vibrant.

Nevertheless, the moment we see happiness as an objective experience after the fact, we make an object of it and want it to reappear in an identical manner. However, this will never happen because it is always different. On the other hand, it is manifesting itself all the time. We cannot tell happiness where and how to manifest itself. God knows best what we need, where to appear, when to appear, and how to appear.

The one who refers to these past experiences is the one who still has the nostalgia. It is the same illusion. That which remains when this illusion is seen for what it is, is God.

It is important not to identify with past experiences, especially with past spiritual experiences. On the whole one should refrain from talking about them or even thinking about them. Every time we think of such an experience, we should immediately understand that the happiness that was present then, is still present now. Use it as a means of coming back to the present, of forgetting the past. Otherwise we create an ego that allegedly had these experiences and, the bigger the experience, the bigger the ego.

The truth we are referring to is peace. It is an absence of problems. It is the true background. It doesn't have this vibrancy, this extraordinary knowledge. It manifests it, but it is not it. This expanded state of consciousness appears in the Self, in peace. It is a different mode of knowing. It is unusual but it is not the source. The source is beyond all of that and is always present.

If we focus our mind on these big experiences, it prevents us from seeing the leaf on the tree, the problem in our neighbor's heart, the sky, the stars, the sun dancing on the wallpaper in our room, and so on—all these little things that tell us about God. Krishnamurti used to say that if we want it big, we don't really want the divine. We cannot see how divine the hills and the mountains are, so we want an angel with wings on top of them.

Is the purpose of awakening to point to the now, where we are?

Yes.

But if one is fortunate enough to have these big experiences, is it still the now?

If we have an experience of happiness, at the moment of happiness itself we are beyond the mind, beyond time. We are in our timeless presence. We are abiding as the Self. This place is the now, the timeless now. It is present right here and now. When the memory of a past experience comes to us, let's say a happy past experience, we welcome it and, in this welcoming, all the objective elements that remain will dissolve and leave us with that which is always present, the perfume. As long as we make an object of this experience, instead of taking advantage of its liberating effect, it binds us still further.

What are these kind of experiences pointing to? Are they pointing just to the Self, to something beyond time?

It is for the one who has these experiences to know where they are pointing. Ultimately, they point to the source, happiness, the Self. However, a general statement could be made about these experiences. In this process of pointing towards the source, towards the Self, they will unravel and reveal some of the complexities of the mind and some contractions in the body. They will free some knots. In that moment, we feel a great relief from these knots. We feel liberated. It is an exhilarating experience. They will also bring understanding, because the moment we have an experience beyond the mind we realize there is a force behind it and that we are this force. If we truly have an experience of being beyond the mind, then there is no death for us any longer.

What about loving other people?

Loving other people is not loving. When there are no others, then there is the possibility of love. It is the only prerequisite. It is a necessary and sufficient condition for love.

℘

In the Indian tradition, it is said that one should stick with one teacher. Would it be wrong then to visit other teachers?

I don't like these "shoulds" and "shouldn'ts." How do they accord with freedom? We should be free from them. However, having said that, it is true to say that in many cases the desire for a teacher arises at some point. Then, like in ancient China, we start touring the mountains. We go from here to there and at each place there is some kind of a teacher. We visit them and at some point think, "I would like to spend some time with this one." However, it is not in fact our decision. It is a decision we do not have to take. It will be taken for us in the heart. However, all of that is an illusion because in reality there is only one teacher.

The teaching in words is just the beginning. After this there is the teaching in silence, which involves simply sitting in the presence of the teacher. However, there is an even higher and more direct form of teaching, which is simply hanging around the teacher.

There is a Hassidic story about an advanced truth seeker who went to see the rabbi, the teacher. The teacher's assistant asked him, "Why do you want to see the master? Do you have any questions you want to ask him?" The truth seeker replied, "No." "Well then, I suppose you want to sit silently in his company and take advantage of the grace that pours from his presence." Again he said, "No." Then the assistant asked, "Well then, what is it that you want?" and the man replied, "I want to see how he puts on his shoes!"

In this business of being a student of the truth, one should feel very free and follow one's heart. Also follow your reason and try to make them work together. If they disagree, follow your heart.

Consciousness and the disciple are one. One should follow love and happiness more than the mind. Follow freedom. One should go to a teacher in whom there is no restriction. For example, in one of his books Jean Klein describes a time before he went to India when he stayed for a while in Sri Lanka. During his stay he became acquainted with the head monk of the Theravadin Buddhist order. They became friends and apparently this monk wanted Jean to stay with him and become his disciple, although he didn't say so at the time. Jean then went to India and wrote him a thank you letter. Sometime later he was surprised to receive a reply from this high-ranking monk, telling him that he was coming to India to visit him. At that time Jean was staying with an Indian friend who was a singer and when the monk arrived, she was in the middle of a recital. So Jean went out to welcome him and said, "Please come in, there is a beautiful recital going on." However, the monk said he could not, because it was against the rules of his order. Jean said,

112

"Well, I respected that, but at the same time I felt it was not my path, because there was some restriction. There was a lack of freedom."

It is important that everything is included: beauty, love, intelligence, and life. Life is a celebration. Consider everything that makes you happy as a gift from God and say, "Thank you." Feel gratitude for being alive, for being conscious, for having been given this extraordinary gift of life, and for being able to look for your true nature.

In this celebration we very often experience great magnificence, enormous potential, when it seems anything could happen. One looks around like a child and thinks that it could be this, that, or anything.

Yes.

I suppose it's linked to the, "What do I do next?" idea, to the sense that with all of this potential.

This is a false question. Ask yourself, "Who is asking the question? Who is this 'I' who doesn't know what to do next?" There is nobody. However, life will move on anyway, don't worry!

I realize it is a false question, but it keeps recurring.

Life will move on. Don't you already have enough activities with a family, children, and your search for the truth? Each moment takes care of itself. It is beautiful to live without knowing what the next moment is going to be, to be open to all this possibility, as you mentioned, like a child. Don't be afraid of this openness. Don't try to fill it! Keep it open!

It is a fear of being stuck that I'm worried about.

Keep everything up in the air. Keep everything open and live from openness to openness.

There seems to be such a gulf between the teacher and the student.

The teacher may seem to be one step ahead. We think we have understood something and indeed we may have done so. However, there is a tendency to crystallize this understanding, to formulate it, and this creates an understander, an ego, a fixed view of how things are. Although the teacher may have formulated the same understanding that enabled us to have a glimpse of our true nature in the first place, nevertheless, when we next approach him, the teaching he gives will be completely new and fresh. Immediately our formulation is dissolved and we are taken to a deeper level of understanding.

As this cycle of formulation and dissolution continues, we may develop a great love for the teacher who is instigating the process. This love is very precious, but a good teacher, which means in this case, one who is completely impersonal, will not let this love be directed towards himself as a person. He will be like a slippery fish, impossible to get hold of or settle onto. This enables the student to see that what he really loves is understanding, intelligence, consciousness, and not a person.

At this point it is possible for the true relationship with the teacher to begin. It is a relationship of impersonal love. As this relationship unfolds we become increasingly sensitive to the obstacles that prevent this meeting in the heart, this impersonal intimacy. It is simply by becoming aware of these obstacles that they begin to drop away, not only in relation to our teacher, although for many of us this may be our first experience of it, but also with others, with our partner, our family, our friends, our colleagues. And strangely enough we find that the more we behave towards others with this attitude of impersonal love, so this attitude in turn compels the other to respond in a similar way. We find that we no longer have problematic relationships.

114

Many traditions refer to surrendering at the feet of the guru. If the real guru is this impersonal presence and not a physical person, what is really meant by "the feet of the guru"?

Meditation is the constant offering of our hopes, fears, beliefs, disbeliefs, doubts, thoughts, feelings, concerns, and world perceptions to the guru, to the conscious presence. It is a constant prasad, a constant giving and receiving. We place all our hopes and fears, our problems, joys, and sorrows at the feet of the guru. The "feet of the guru" is the threshold of consciousness, this place in the mind that doesn't belong to the mind, this openness, this window through which consciousness sees the mind. It is this conscious presence in us.

This offering is not something that we do once and for all. It is a continuous offering to the threshold from moment to moment. It is from the same threshold to which we offer, that we receive. However, we cannot receive if our hands are full of objects. So we have to give, to offer, in order to be empty-handed, empty-minded. We have to be in not-knowing in order to receive the gift from the guru, the grace, the understanding, the presence, the life. As long as we hold onto the problem or try to solve the problem, there is no offering. There is no not-knowing.

Offer your thoughts especially. Let the universe take care of the problem. If your thoughts are running in circles, just offer them to the infinite. This will break the circle of your repetitive thoughts so that you can be graced with intuition and understanding.

Let the emptiness pervade your mind and your body. Offer body, mind and world to the presence constantly. As soon as you realize that you are stuck, gently liberate yourself from the stickiness. It is not an effort. In fact, it is the ending of an effort. Don't make an effort out of it. It is a relief to let go. If you make an effort you pile up an effort on top of a pre-existing effort. This is not what "letting go" means. Give it back to the infinite. Let the infinite take care of it. You don't have to carry the weight.

115

At a certain stage in meditation, it is mostly your body that appears, so your body naturally becomes the principal object of your contemplation. At this stage, the principal offering to consciousness is the body with all its feelings and sensations.

Be willing to completely lose control over the body, over the feelings. It is our will to make things happen, to play God, little god, that prevents them from happening, that gets in the way of the natural flow of things. Understand that you are not in control of anything, that there is no choice you make as an individual, no decision.

Let your experience of the body be whatever it wants to be, however it spontaneously evolves. Trust this unknowing. Do not be attached to any image of the body. Become aware of all of the tensions that have been superimposed onto our natural emptiness and which have thereby created a separate entity or the illusion of a separate entity. Do not try to eliminate these contractions but don't reject them either. Give them complete freedom to evolve in space and time.

There is no goal, nothing to achieve, no need for striving. Consciousness is already a fact. It is the most basic of all facts. It doesn't have to be brought in. It is already here and everything is in it. So why strive? And what is it that we are striving for? We can only strive for an object, something of no value.

Instead of striving, contemplate the striving. Welcome your striving. Let it tell its story. Simply love, simply welcome the striving. Welcome the striving mind and the striving body without striving for them to be different in any way from what they are.

8

An Explosion of Freedom

I have had occasional experience of meeting someone when there is no them or me, but all day long we are busy meeting people. Can you say something about that?

The only place that we can start from is our own experience, not somebody else's. We have to research the true nature of our being and understand first that there is nobody here. That is the prerequisite. At some point we understand that what we truly are, is this non-localized presence, non-localized welcoming. At the very moment we understand this, we have a glimpse of it, because we can only understand it when we are it. To understand it we need to be it knowingly and, at that moment, we become acquainted with the impersonal way of being, of just being present without being a person; being open, being this welcoming space.

This welcoming space is not only a welcoming mind, a mind that is open to other people, their ideas, concepts, and concerns, but it is also a welcoming body. A welcoming body is a body that is not solid, not limited, but which is open to the totality, completely vulnerable. When another person appears in this welcoming space, the welcoming presence is felt by the other as friendliness, as silence, as very intimate. The other feels you as family and rightfully so, because what is being felt is his or her own intimacy at that moment, which is the space of silence that we share. In other words, our being silent and welcoming in this way resonates through the screen of thoughts and feelings, and goes directly to this place which we have, which we are, in common.

In India there are various ways of classifying these means of transmission, such as through silence, looking, speaking, and touching. This experience of oneness has various ways of communicating and expressing itself. It comes in different flavors, but it comes from the same place and it takes us to the same place.

Everything that comes from love is spontaneous. Spontaneous means the absence of a person, a separate entity. For example, if while looking at someone, the thought comes to us that what is behind their eyes is our own essence, and if we treat this person accordingly, our subsequent behavior will be spontaneous. It may look like a doing but it is not. It comes from understanding. Everything that comes from understanding is spontaneous.

If someone who has many layers of protection, and therefore many conflicts, approaches us, enters our field of expansion, we will feel their tensions in ourself. These tensions are not something that we are carrying around. They come to us from the circumstances. If we welcome them completely, they will flow through us and, at the same time, we are very subtly showing the other person the way out of his or her problems. This other person won't realize it, perhaps they will never understand what has happened, but it is very efficient.

What is the true purpose of our existence?

Happiness. We are born out of happiness and are an expression of happiness. We are also an instrument that is very well designed to find happiness. We are an instrument of celebration.

118

I see that I create my own problems, but I do not see others as myself. It doesn't worry me. Should I just carry on?

Of course. Carry on as long as you are happy. The purpose of life is to find happiness and to celebrate it, so whatever makes you truly happy is perfect.

I have been told that I am self-realized but do not know it.

We project the state of self-realization and we project a "someone" who is in that state. The reason that we project "someone" being in a state of self-realization is because we project ourselves as a "someone" being in a state of non-realization. We should ask ourselves, "Who is there to be realized or non-realized?"

What is the flash of enlightenment that the Upanishads speak of?

Some of the teachings in the Upanishads are nearer the mark than others. The ancient sages were addressing people with problems, people who took themselves for individuals, and they would therefore answer their questions from the individual's vantage point, the vantage point of ignorance. From that vantage point there are realized and non-realized beings. The people who were asking the questions didn't immediately want the ultimate truth, though the sages tried to take them there directly. Therefore, the sages granted them their point of view in a provisional way and answered accordingly. We have to understand that these people's point of view was mistaken. Here we are more drastic. The question is, "Am I a separate individual?"

Realization, when it is understood as an event in time, would mean that something had been added, that something was not present before, that something had come in. However, from where would it come and for whom?

Then would it be useful to keep in mind the question, "What am I?"

It is not necessary to keep it in mind. However, when circumstances that bring about suffering arise in daily life, we should investigate, "What is it or who is it that is suffering?" When we are happy, however, there is no need to ask, "Who is happy?" Just be happy. When you are happy you are in your true state, because the true purpose of life is happiness, which is something we all know. That is why all human beings are looking for happiness. Happiness is not the question, it is the answer. The answer is not a verbal response. It is life itself. It is consciousness itself. It is you. It is your very being.

ᘓ

If I completely give up my identification as I go to sleep, how is it that this identification seems to come back again in the morning?

This question is based on an illusion, on the fallacy of a personal entity that would give up its personal identification and get it back again when it wakes up. This entity itself is an illusion. In fact the reason why there is ignorance and the apparent waking up from it, is simply divine pleasure, divine play. It is a game that we are playing with ourselves. We are children at play.

When we fall deeply asleep, we experience peace. We go back to peace every night and also in between thoughts in the waking state. If we are attracted by the interval between two thoughts, if we want to abide in it, then it becomes an experience. It is not an objective experience, but it is an experience nevertheless. This interval of peace between two thoughts, which seems to be an illusion from the vantage point of the mind, becomes a reality. This is also true of the interval between two perceptions or two sensations. As this experience deepens, the so-called reality of the world correspondingly loses its tangibility; that is, it loses its reality as something outside and separate from consciousness.

Is there a difference between enlightenment and self-realization?

Enlightenment and self-realization are different. Enlightenment is the actual understanding that consciousness is not personal. It is the experience of the timelessness, impersonality, and limitlessness of consciousness. The seed of enlightenment is the feeling of being attracted by the truth, being interested in the truth. This seed is planted by grace. Self-realization is the establishment of this understanding at all levels of our experience, our thinking, feeling, and perceiving. It implies that at some point we find that we have no problems, we enjoy life to its fullest.

It is possible that others will use these words in different ways and that is fine. In fact it is good. It teaches us not to ascribe any absolute value to anything apart from the Absolute. We shouldn't worry about the meaning of words. It is what they signify that is important.

I have trouble with the idea of disappearing.

The person is afraid of disappearing or, more accurately, the person *is* the fear of disappearing. However, that which we are, consciousness, has no trouble with it because it knows deeply that it never disappears. There comes a moment when we feel a great freedom in ourselves, freedom from death. This enables us to truly live life to the fullest, whatever that means for each of us, for the expressions of beauty, love, and intelligence are so diverse.

There is nobody who becomes self-realized. The notion of someone becoming self-realized is a contradiction of terms. We should not think of ourself, or anybody else, in terms of being realized or not. It would be better to use expressions such as, "This person is a beautiful human being." Or just state the facts such as, "When I am with this person I feel good, I don't feel fear and, if I do, it is just an old mechanism that doesn't last, it just vanishes and my sky is blue again." Or, "I feel that I have become a truth lover and that is the only thing that matters in my life." All we can do is find who we are, rest there, and celebrate. There is nothing to worry about.

121

What about attempting to celebrate from an ignorant viewpoint, thinking that we are resting there?

Celebration is spontaneous. It comes from joy itself. Contrived celebration is not celebration. True celebration comes on the spot. It has its own flavor. It doesn't come from the feeling, "I have realized." That would be the wrong premise. True celebration doesn't have any explanations, any verbalizations associated with it. It is just an explosion of freedom. When we are here together, there are moments when we feel this sweetness, like family. When we feel this perfume, that is the celebration.

If we believe that the perfume is an object, we will never find it and we will claim that it is missing. However, this perfume cannot be absent. That which can be absent is not the true perfume. All we have to do is to get rid of the notion that it is not present. If we entertain the notion that it is not present, we then go looking for it, and the more we look for it the less we experience it. Get rid of the notion that it is somewhere else, that we have to struggle for it, that we have to pay a price for it, that we have to suffer for it, that we have to make efforts. Life doesn't need to be different. We can live a normal life. It is OK to work, to make money, to make life easy for ourselves and for our family. Everything is OK.

Sometimes things have gone wrong and our innocence seems to be betrayed.

We have to understand, and this usually happens in retrospect, that it is precisely this betrayal of innocence that has led us to innocence. See that every event in our life was exactly what was needed at the moment it occurred, in order to keep us on the track that led us to the truth, that led us to innocence. Those circumstances provided just the right impetus towards truth; otherwise we would have remained static. To think that our innocence has been betrayed, betrays our way of thinking. There is in fact only innocence in motion towards innocence at rest.

122

Somebody once asked Jean Klein about a child of four years old who died, and he answered, "How do you know that those four years weren't exactly the right amount of time he needed in order to know absolute happiness?"

Some of us feel that death is the ultimate abomination, but it is just our conditioning that makes us see it that way. We have to understand that as long as we look at the world as a human being, as a separate individual, we will see things accordingly, but as soon as we look at it from the vantage point of consciousness, it is quite different.

୪

What can one do about ego?

We have to understand what "ego" means. I use the word "ego" in a very precise way, which is different from the way it is used in psychology. I use it to refer to any thought or feeling that identifies consciousness exclusively with the body-mind organism. In fact, it is almost a synonym of ignorance, which is a better term, because it has nothing to do with the individual characteristics of the separate body-mind. Ignorance is the belief that consciousness is somehow dependent on the body-mind for its existence. That is ignorance or ego. It is a thought or a feeling. It is important to understand this, and not to think that the ego is an entity.

An example of ego is the thought or the feeling, "I am something," "I am a woman," "I am a human being," "I am happy," "I am this age," and so on. It is important to see that, because if we say, "Ego is an illusion," people sometimes misunderstand this and say, "I perceive my mind, body, and thoughts, and yet you are telling me that I don't exist." This is not what is meant. What is meant is that it is an illusion to think that what we are is a thought or a feeling or an entity.

123

The second common mistake is to think that the ego is something that we have to get rid of, or that we have to get rid of individuality. There is nothing wrong with the mind or the body. They do not need to be changed. It is the mistaken identity that gets corrected, the misunderstanding that we, consciousness, are dependent on the body-mind, which suggests that if the body dies, the mind dies, and if the mind dies, consciousness dies. That is ignorance.

What is the difference between individuality and ego?

Individuality is each unique manifestation of consciousness in human form. Ego is the feeling or belief that what we call "I," consciousness, is exclusively limited to and dependent on one of these forms. Individuality is a celebration of the Self. Ego is an apparent limitation of it.

All that needs to be done is to see the situation clearly. We get rid of misunderstanding through understanding, not through violence, effort, or belief. The ego is a misunderstanding, so freeing ourselves from ego can only take place through understanding. Understanding comes as a result of the investigation into the true nature of Self, self-inquiry. Only intelligence and understanding can free us from the false notion that is the source of our misery. Once the wrong perspective has been readjusted, then everything else gradually falls back into place, into its organic position.

The investigation that precedes this understanding is not made through effort. It is enjoyable. We should only do it if we are interested in it, if the question invites us, in which case we should allow ourselves to be invited. If we are invited, at the level of thoughts or bodily feelings, by the question, "Who am I?" then say, "Yes." Cooperate, but no effort, no conflict. Conflict and effort only perpetuate the original mistake. It is better just to keep this attitude of freedom, of free thinking.

Intellectual understanding can go very deep, but we then have to live in accordance with this understanding. It has to expand into all realms of our life, daily activity, professional life, relationships, the way we feel our body, our understanding of beauty, and so on. When we are in love with truth, we are eager to cooperate with this expansion, so that all realms of life become an opportunity for celebration. We don't want to be happy only when we think.

Patanjali refers to two sorts of "I-ness."

There are two sorts of I-thought. The first is when we think "I" without any attribute or limitation, without any image, without attaching the I-thought to anything, such as, "I am a person." This pure I-thought refers directly to consciousness, but it is still an object because it is a thought. However, this thought takes us directly to its referent, which is consciousness. This I-thought is not ignorant although it is not consciousness. It refers directly to the source. This is what is meant by, "'I' is the first name of God."

The second I-thought is the identified I-thought, the ego. For example, "I am a human being," "I am a man," "I am a woman," and so on. At the moment this thought appears, ignorance takes birth. The pure I-thought is really a bridge between its referent, consciousness, and ignorance. It is a gate. It is for this reason that Christ said, "'I' is the way, 'I' is the truth, 'I' is life." The bridge that we cross one way going out of the Garden of Eden can be crossed the other way going back. The place of "I am-ness" is the beacon that tells us where the Golden Gate is.

"I" as a thought can be seen as untrue, but "I" as a feeling doesn't seem quite the same.

In both cases it is an object, an appearance, something manifested. It appears to consciousness. The question arises, "Am I that which appears or that to which it appears? What am I?"

When the I-feeling appears, it appears to me, whatever that is. This I-feeling, which is an object, is not the real "I," because I am the real "I" to which it appears. I am the witness, not the witnessed.

This witness is not the ego. The ego is the I-feeling identified, or the I-thought identified. It is the feeling, "I am located here in this body." Or it is the thought, "I am this body, I am this person." The pure I-feeling is beyond the ego. The reason we call it pure is because it is not identified. It has been separated from attributes.

In order to understand that I am the witness and not the witnessed I-feeling or the I-thought, I must somehow have the experience of the witness; otherwise, I couldn't possibly understand that. This understanding comes directly from the experience of the source. This understanding *is* in fact the experience of the source. It is a glimpse of our true nature. It is nowhere and everywhere. It is nowhere because it is not an object, it is not in space. It is everywhere because all objects appear in it.

Could you say something about using the thought "I" or "I am" as a way of returning to one's true nature? I find it very difficult.

It doesn't matter if you don't know how to focus on "I am." Just try it. To try it is to be successful. As you try it, you will recognize it, because you know what you are. You know the direction of the "I am." It knows itself in you. Don't stop at any object, any thought or feeling. Gently take the attention away from this thought or feeling back to the "I am."

At first it might feel like an effort. Let this effort relax back into the source or the Self, which it is seeking. Keep the intensity, but let this intensity lose its contour, its contraction. Every time you get stuck with a sensation, a feeling, or a thought, think or feel "I" inside. Focus the attention on the deep feeling of "I." That will unstick you. Although the one who meditates on the Self looks very quiet from the outside, there is in fact a great intensity inside. There is a great intensity of desire, of turning the attention towards the source.

Feelings, thoughts, and perceptions are not rejected in this meditation. They appear in the perfume of "I-am-ness." The attention is not directed towards them, but rather towards the "I-am-ness." The one who is afraid, the one who desires, the one who likes and dislikes, is a mere body-mind appearance against the background of "I-am-ness." Don't lose sight of the background. Don't feel you are unsuccessful in this meditation. You are successful every time you redirect the attention towards its source.

From the thought "I," we go to a more subtle feeling, the I-feeling. And from there, it merges with the Absolute, with its source. It merges with the source of our intention, this presence, this all-pervading conscious space, this "I am."

The problem we sometimes encounter in trying to do this is that either the conscious space or the thought "I" may remain as objects. The space may remain a physical space or a space in the mind, without merging with presence. The conscious space, the all-pervading consciousness, and the "I am" are all the same thing, which is not a thing.

However, this unique thing can be approached from two different angles. One is from feeling, from open space, open welcoming. The other is from the I-thought, and this is closer to the mind, to the inner world.

In both cases we may encounter dryness at some point, a lack of perfume. In this case, it would be interesting to try the other tool, knowing that they are ultimately the same. It is simply a different version of the same vehicle. In this way we return to an experience of presence that is vibrant. It is not a blank state.

As we take the I-thought, we take it with the intention of understanding, of experiencing the reality that it refers to. We take this I-thought and we allow it to guide us to the source, and then we abide in this source for a few moments. To begin with, the habit of agitation in the mind or in the body, will take us away. At that moment, we can again gently take this I-thought, always in a living way, with a desire to experience its referent, our presence.

"I" is the highest mantra. In using it in this way, we avoid boring repetitions. It always remains alive, always directed towards its meaning. Just try it and be very determined, courageous, patient, and stubborn at the same time. Make sure that the juice, the perfume, is always flowing. Make sure you are not simply singing the song without understanding the meaning.

We don't have to repeat the thought "I" unless we realize we have lost the feeling of presence. We use the thought "I" as a reminder, as a line that takes us back to safety, whenever we discover we are lost. In this way we also avoid monotonous repetition. When we are abiding in presence, it is unnecessary to say "I." The "I" mantra is only used in the presence of dryness, doubt, or lack.

This "I" mantra is also the shortest form of highest reasoning, the shortest thought that takes us back to understanding, to intelligence. Once that has been understood we realize that, just as it supersedes all mantras, it also supersedes all clever means that can be used by the mind. In other words, once that has been understood, there is no need for any further thought. In this case, if there is a thought or a feeling, we simply release this thought or this feeling into the "I am-ness."

Could you say more about these two different ways of going to our true nature, one through thinking and the other through feeling, and the obstacles that we encounter?

Whenever you notice that you are involved in thinkingness, just notice it. Don't judge yourself. There is nobody to be judged. It is just a natural phenomenon arising. Similarly your recognition of it is another natural phenomenon. There is nobody to judge or be judged. Surrender both the judge and the judged to the presence in which they appear.

Live with whatever the moment brings, fresh and new. Let it flow through you, allowing each appearance to be freely replaced with the next appearance. Don't stick to any appearance. The fall from the Garden of Eden takes place when we become attracted by and involved with objects, forgetting our true center, the presence. When we stick to objects, either because we want to keep them or because we want to get rid of them, we fall from the garden. The objects are the devil's temptation. We go back to the garden when we unstick ourselves from objects.

At the level of bodily sensation, we may find ourselves stuck with a big feeling or a big sensation. Usually this is because, implicitly or explicitly, we want to get rid of it and we are therefore consciously or unconsciously focusing on it. In this way, our attention becomes captive of this particular feeling. We have fallen into the devil's trap. Simply recognizing that we have fallen into the trap, liberates us from it.

If there is thinkingness, let it find its own resolution. Its momentum will dissipate simply by no longer fueling this dynamism. It is like riding uphill on a bicycle: if you stop making any effort, the momentum wears off and you come to a stop. It is the same here. Stop adding energy to the thinking process by believing in the myth of a separate being.

When the agitation of thought diminishes, the feeling level becomes more apparent. This is the time to be courageous because some feelings that come up may be overwhelming. However, they are only feelings. They are in fact only bodily sensations with a "me" attached to them. If we quietly let them do their thing, the "me" level detaches itself. They lose their "me-ness" and also, by the same token, their meanness. They become more docile, tamed, presentable, civilized. They are no longer a problem. We can live with them. We can have a life in spite of them.

The main obstacle is to want to get rid of these feelings, to eliminate them. That is the trap of the gradual path. It is endless. The moment we become hypnotized by a feeling as a result of wanting to get rid of it, we are stuck. We remain stuck at that level until we let go of the desire to get rid of it. We can stay there for years or for a split second, which is the same as not staying there at all. It is our choice. If we get stuck for a long time with every feeling we encounter, the path is endless. Understand that it is truly our choice whether or not we get stuck with every feeling we encounter. It is not something that is imposed upon us. It is something we impose upon ourselves. We do it because we like it. For instance, if someone is angry and wants to perpetuate his anger and act it out, it is simply because he or she enjoys it.

In meditation, everything is magnified. Everything is under the microscope. Everything becomes more evident, because we are in the laboratory.

It is such relief when we enter the direct path, when we finally give up trying to get rid of feelings, because it is so much work. We don't have to do anything about these feelings. We can divorce them at any time. In fact we are not even married to them. When we understand this, we realize by the same token that we don't have to go feeling by feeling. We can give them up, surrender them, in bulk, wholesale, and just remain in beingness. If the feelings are present, they are present. If they want to leave, they leave. We have nothing to do with them, no agenda. We remain in beingness.

Beingness is a different world, a different dimension, to which feelings have no access. That is why any manipulation of the feelings can never take us to beingness. Just as we can cut through thinkingness and go directly to the underlying feeling, so we can cut right through the layer of feelingness, boldly, and return to beingness. Take your stand as awareness, no matter what.

If we take our stand in beingness there will usually be great upheaval to begin with. There will be a revolt, an uproar. However, stay strong, bold, and steady because at the end the feelings lose. Gradually and miraculously things will sort themselves out.

The moment we take our stand in beingness, we open the gates of harmony. To begin with there is a lot of pressure. There is a big flow of energy through these gates, but the flow is moving in the right direction. Don't be disappointed if you think you are not getting the expected objective result. That is not the way it happens. The results don't come from the objects. Being is a different world, a different dimension.

You mentioned earlier the tendency to get stuck in this process of returning to the source.

There are two principle ways of becoming stuck at an intermediary level: one is due to passivity, the other is due to activity. Passivity, laziness, or apathy takes place when we discover a thought or a feeling

130

that we do not really want to see. In order to cover it up, we create some sort of daydream, some sort of mental activity. This takes us away from the problem, from the tension, from the contraction. It is a refusal, an escape.

Activity or agitation takes place at a later stage. This occurs when we want to eliminate the problem rather than escape it. The desire to eliminate the problem sticks us to it. Although it is a higher level than refusing to experience the thought or feeling fully, it is still a level of stickiness.

We can be stuck for years with one single problem, either in passivity or activity. It is important to see that clearly, so that we can implement this understanding in our meditation, so that we don't waste our time at those intermediary levels.

Beingness is ever-present and permeates all things. Even hell wouldn't exist without the beingness that permeates it. No matter what the feeling, we have the freedom to go back to this beingness in a split second. We can divorce the feelingness and the thinkingness, divorce our infatuation with a separate entity whenever we truly want to, provided we face the music that ensues with determination.

You talk about fear arising at some point.

The ego is surrounded by fear and desire. The ego is at the center of the web and the web is made of fear and desire. At the core of the web is the I-thought and the I-feeling. Whenever we become aware of fear it is like saying, "I am in the web." If we follow the web to its center, we end up at the spider. It is the same here: if we follow the fear, at some point we arrive at the ego, the thought or feeling that I, consciousness, is limited. At that moment the ego is defenseless. Just seeing it for what it is accomplishes its disappearance or at least its disempowerment because, being itself a misunderstanding, it cannot tolerate being seen clearly, being understood. When there is no longer a spider at the center, the web is irreparably damaged and can no longer be fixed or expanded. We cooperate with this process by simply knowing that whenever we get entangled in the web, it doesn't really matter because there is in fact no spider at the center that can harm us.

After we have seen the root of fear, the ego, the fundamental mistake, it doesn't necessarily imply that fear has disappeared altogether. The residual web is still present and we may occasionally get entangled in it, but the situation now is very different, because we see clearly that there is no danger of being killed by the spider. So we disentangle ourselves and that destroys a portion of the web. The more the web is eliminated, the more freely we move around.

We can never be sure that there isn't some little piece of web remaining, but it doesn't matter. We enjoy ourselves dancing around and celebrating. Any fear is just a pale reflection of what it used to be; it has lost its power. In the beginning we get entangled a lot because the spider is still apparently present, but after some time the web has been pretty much destroyed.

When the web appears and we get entangled in it, we shouldn't be afraid of the spider. It doesn't matter whether the spider has been neutralized already or whether it is still active, because in both cases it cannot hurt us. It is only the belief that the spider can hurt us that is dangerous. The ego spider is in fact powerless. Whenever we get entangled in the web, we should completely welcome this entanglement. Don't resist it.

We get to the spider by having no intention to go anywhere and simply welcoming the entanglement or the predicament in which we find ourselves. By welcoming a piece of the web, we are led to the spider. As we get closer to the spider, fear increases and then at some point we decide that, come what may, we will keep welcoming out of love for truth. Then we reach the spider and look it in the eyes, and that kills it. So don't worry about the entanglements.

However, if you are asking how to be free of unpleasantness, the answer is, "See your freedom." You are free. It is only the illusion, the thought, the belief that we are not free that binds us. Consciousness is freedom itself.

9

What the Mind Cannot Know

Some sensations are unpleasant. What changes when I know that I am not a sensation?

An unpleasant sensation is made of two components, the sensation itself and its unpleasantness. It is the unpleasantness that is the problem. The unpleasantness is the reaction of a "someone" for whom the sensation is unpleasant. The "someone" is the reaction, the resistance, the "I don't like." This reaction, this dislike, is itself another sensation. So there are two sensations.

We are not trying to understand that we are not the first sensation, we are trying to investigate for whom the first sensation is unpleasant. If we completely welcome this unpleasantness, this resistance, we realize that we are the space in which it appears, that we are not whatever is being welcomed. In this way we automatically experience ourselves as the witnessing presence in which the sensation, the reaction against it, and its alleged reacting subject, the ego, appear.

We should welcome the whole situation, the sensation and our resistance to it. If the resistance is itself unpleasant, then welcome this third sensation and so on. If we pile up sensations in this way, at some point there is no further resistance and we start to move in

133

the opposite direction. This time, all the superimposed resistances eliminate themselves as we go, and we get back to the first sensation, but this time without the resistance. In this way, the unpleasantness of the original sensation vanishes, and we give it the freedom to unfold and reveal its true nature. Usually, we don't have to go far up the pile. It is enough to welcome the first resistance, to see that there is a resistance. To be aware of the resistance enables us to understand that we are not the resisting ego, that we are simply the witnessing presence in which the sensation and the resistance appear. We discover that there is nobody resisting, that the resistance and the one who dislikes are one and the same. There is nobody who dislikes other than the dislike itself.

Having preferences and aversions seems to be permanent.

No, we have many neutral moments. Even if it were true that we move from like to dislike, then, when the like is present, the dislike is not present and vice versa, so neither is permanent. Since they are not permanent, they are not an intrinsic part of consciousness. Consciousness neither likes nor dislikes, although all likes and dislikes appear in it.

You said that happiness is related to universal consciousness. I understand consciousness, but I do not understand the universality of it.

The greatest certainty we can have is that we are conscious. In fact, it is the only certainty we can have. Just ask yourself, "Am I conscious now?" or, "Is consciousness present now?" Even though we don't know what consciousness is, we know that the answer to that question is, "Yes." That to which we refer in order to answer, "Yes," is what we call consciousness. It is not an objective experience, but nevertheless we are absolutely certain of it.

Just the fact that we see and understand these words shows that what we call consciousness is present, for how could we see or understand them if something wasn't present to experience them? That "something" is what we call consciousness.

The next question to ask is, "Is this consciousness, whatever it is, personal, limited?" If we claim that it is limited, by the same token we imply that we are aware of its limitations, otherwise we could not legitimately make the claim. In this case that which is aware of the limitations would itself be what we call consciousness.

As long as we think that consciousness is individual, a belief system is still present. When we don't know, we are open to the discovery of happiness. As long as these beliefs are present there will be reactions piled up one on top of another. These reactions occur because we are looking at things from the point of view of a body-mind, not from universal consciousness.

We have to investigate whether we have any actual experience of separation. There is certainly an experience of consciousness, right now and always. The mind will never know it in the same way it knows that two plus two equals four, in an objective way. However, we may know it in a different way, in identity, in the way that we know when we understand something, in a glimpse, or when we know that we are conscious. Since being conscious is not an objective experience we might ask ourselves, "How do I know that I am conscious?" Nevertheless, we are absolutely certain that we are conscious.

This knowledge of being conscious is derived from an experience that is not objective. Therefore there is a mode of knowledge that is not phenomenal, which is not objective, and which is beyond the scope of science. If we are open to this mode of knowledge it will reveal itself in a moment of love, understanding, or beauty, and in that moment we are beyond the mind.

For instance, when we communicate, when we have a conversation, there are moments when we are totally certain that we are communicating, that we are understanding each other. We may wonder how it is possible that we are truly talking about the same thing if we are two separate entities. If it is true that we are two separate consciousnesses, we could never be certain that we are talking about the same thing. If this is the case then, when we are communicating, either we are deluding ourselves or, at that moment, we are one single consciousness. If we think deeply about it, it is not possible for two separate consciousnesses to ever be certain that they are understanding each other because, in order to understand, a meeting, a merger, a fusion is required.

Are we deluding ourselves when we think, "I am conscious"? If we take a closer look at those times when we have a moment of understanding, love, or beauty, if we try to find from what experience this comes, we find that it comes from the same non-objective experience, from the same timeless glimpse, as the experience that enables us to say, "I am conscious." This is not phenomenal knowledge, but knowledge in identity, knowledge in being.

CB

It is almost impossible to focus on really intense pain.

I do not recommend focusing on pain. On the contrary, I recommend welcoming it, not piling up resistance against it, opening oneself up to it, but at the same time allowing it to flow. If we focus on it, we block it. Let it flow completely.

My experience is that it is almost impossible to let it flow completely. It takes me over.

Let yourself be taken over and then welcome the reaction. That is all you can do and that's fine. There is a Zen story of a teacher who is dying, subject to tremendous pain. He is screaming and his student asks, "Why are you screaming? Three years ago you had a terrible pain and you did not scream." The teacher replied, "At that time I wasn't dying!" We do whatever we can. Pain and pleasure are part of this body package.

At a moment of intense pain everything is abandoned.

Such an experience calls for total presence in the moment. In fact it leads us to the moment. We don't have much room to think other than to think nothing.

136

In the moment it is what it is.

Consciousness is witnessing whatever it is. The very fact that we can speak about it shows that we are the witness of it. It is a very intense experience. In the tantra, an intense experience is said to be a very good opportunity for enlightenment, because it is a big buildup of energy. We just follow it, wherever it leads. Intense pleasure or intense pain are equally valid. If we eliminate the like and dislike part and take only the intensity of it they are not that different.

What do you mean by welcoming intense anger and frustration, as well as the hatred of it?

There is the expression of anger, the repression of anger, and there is welcoming. Expression is better than repression. Repression is tamasic, dull; it makes us insensitive. Expression is rajasic, it stirs up the passions. To welcome it, to love it, to go to the root of it through love and understanding is harmonious, sattvic.

So should I try not to focus on the child that is driving me mad and just allow these feelings?

We have to understand who it is that is being driven mad. Then, if we feel that it is "me," we have to go deeply into the "me-ness" that is angry. Unless we have cleared up this side of the issue, anger is going to come up again and again out of this source. It is like a bag without a bottom. Anger, fear, and desire will continue to come out of this bag. Therefore when we feel anger, we have to ask ourselves, "Who is it that is angry?" We may start with thoughts like, "But he did that to me, how dare he!" However, after this level of thinking, we have to inquire who is the "me" that we are talking about. It is a feeling. "Me" will become a feeling, not just a thought. Then we have to investigate this feeling completely.

It is important to see that we normally want to get rid of this angry reaction. Who wants to get rid of the reaction? It is the same "me." Unless we investigate this situation, we will be caught endlessly in a cycle of reactivity and the desire to get rid of it. The same is true if our inquiry is motivated by a desire to change anything. We have to understand that the one who is angry and the one who wants to get rid of the anger are one and the same.

We have to go deeply into the feeling of "me" when it comes up. When we are perfectly happy it is not necessary to do that, but when we feel a sense of lack, a sense of misery, a problem, then we should investigate deeply who it is that is miserable at that moment. Go into it deeply. It is a feeling.

This "me-ness" is a perceived thing, like a seed. Let it grow completely, like a tree, and ask yourself, "Who is the true 'me'? Is it the tree which is being witnessed or the consciousness in which it is appearing?"

If we welcome the anger completely it will either dissolve or lead us to this "me" again, and then we keep welcoming. We love our anger; we let it come out. We start with a little anger inside, then we may discover huge anger, frustration, fear and then, at the root of it, there is this ultimate fear.

ଓ

What is the mind?

It is a question of definition. I define the mind as thought, perception, and sensation. It is a general term covering everything that it is perceived. It is generally considered to be a bag containing all our hopes, desires, fears, memories, and so on, but in fact we have never experienced such an organ, so we cannot claim that there is such a thing. Our actual experience is a flow of thoughts, sensations, and perceptions. They are not *contained* in the mind; they *are* what we call the mind, and they appear in consciousness. Everything that is perceived is mind stuff, phenomena, appearances, objects, whereas consciousness is the perceiving element, the witness of the mind stuff.

What about understanding?

If understanding is seen as a process, it is usually in two steps. There is a first step that takes place as an ongoing line of thought. This is a process in time, in which various aspects of a question are explored, and then there is a moment of understanding. This moment is timeless. It is instantaneous. This takes place beyond the mind, in a creative moment, in which the exploring thought comes to an end naturally. It leaves us in understanding. We are following the thought and then it dies in its source, which is consciousness.

Therefore understanding takes place when a thought comes to an end. When understanding is present, the thought is not. We cannot say, therefore, that we understand a thought. Understanding has no object. It understands itself. Understanding is one of the ways in which consciousness reveals itself to itself.

Humor is another. When we get a joke, the joke has already vanished. The punch line comes to an end, it disappears, and then we laugh. This moment of humor, when we "get" the joke, is another moment in which consciousness reveals itself to itself. Actually it doesn't take place in a moment. That "moment" is timeless, out of time, but when the mind reappears to formulate the experience, it mistakenly construes it as having taken place at a moment in time.

In fact, when anything is "known," whatever is known ceases to exist as an apparent object and merges with consciousness. That is what knowing is. All we ever truly know is consciousness. Consciousness knows itself in this vast diversity of experience.

Consciousness is intelligence itself. If we approach consciousness with a question, then, when the question dies, we find ourselves in the universal answer. We *are* the answer. All the answers are there in a single moment. If we go to consciousness following a feeling, then, when the feeling dies, the response is love or happiness. Consciousness experiences itself as love or happiness. If we naturally follow a sense perception, then, when it dies, the response from consciousness is beauty. It could be said that understanding is the intellectual aspect of consciousness, love is the feeling aspect of consciousness, and beauty is the perceptual aspect of consciousness.

A work of art is an object composed of various elements, which takes us through this journey of perceptions. It leads us through a medley of thoughts, feelings, and perceptions and, at some point, when we have gone through the various elements, it leaves us in a place of silence.

The mind wants to know, but cannot. When the mind knows that it cannot know, it becomes silent. When the mind becomes silent, when it gives up its pretension of knowing and becomes empty of its entire luggage, we receive from this invisible source that is the core of our being, precisely what needs to be known at every moment, if indeed anything needs to be known. To live in this way, in this silence of the mind, open to the universal harmony, is what is called to live in the Tao. Then there is happiness at every moment, miracle at every moment, discovery, newness, freshness, creation, at every moment. It is very easy. There is no need to be self-realized to have this experience. Just do it.

Could you speak of not being the doer?

The understanding, "I am not the doer," is on the negative side. It is what I am *not*, and it leaves one in a state of resignation. Happiness is still missing. Happiness comes from the experience of what I *am*, not from the understanding of what I am not. The understanding, "I am not the doer," for instance, does not imply the understanding that consciousness is impersonal. This is especially true if the understanding, "I am not the doer," comes from a materialistic view of the world, such as, "I understand that I am not the doer because this mind is the product of the body and this body is a product of the universe, which is itself subject to the law of causality. Therefore any action undertaken by this body is part of the action of the universe."

This understanding, "I am not the doer," is a logical understanding, based on an honest scientific perspective. If, according to this, the mind is dependent on the body and consciousness is dependent on the mind, there will still be the fear of disappearing. There will be the fear of the disappearance of this body, which means the disappearance of this mind, which in turn means disappearance into nothingness. In this case there will be

140

some relaxation, because we understand that there is nothing we can do, but at the same time there will be some resignation because of the lack of joy.

The understanding, "I am not the doer," does not logically imply that consciousness is universal, that my experience of "I am," of being, is universal and eternal. I don't see how there can be happiness under those circumstances. There can be some peace with resignation, but certainly not true celebration. True celebration comes from the good news that there is no death, from the deep feeling that what I am is eternal, not from the intellectual and dry understanding that there is nothing that I can do.

Therefore, "I am not the doer" is not the ultimate understanding, because it does not imply that consciousness is impersonal. Ramana Maharshi discovered that there is no death when his body died at the age of sixteen. He discovered that this "I am-ness" is eternal. Of course the corollary of this is, "I am not this little doer." Therefore, if it is understood as a corollary of a bigger experience, of the experience of silence, of presence, of eternity, it is all right. Having said that, if someone is making efforts, it may be useful to tell this person, "You are not the doer. What are you trying to achieve? It doesn't make any sense since there is no doer." In the cessation of effort that follows, there will be a window of opportunity for a glimpse of our true nature.

What is Sahaja samadhi?

The term Sahaja samadhi is usually used in relation to Nirvikalpa samadhi. Nirvikalpa samadhi is the experience of our true nature. In Nirvikalpa samadhi there is the presence, the knowledge, and the joy of our eternity. The natural process of realization after Nirvikalpa samadhi is Sahaja samadhi. After Nirvikalpa samadhi, after the experience of the ultimate joy, the world reappears and the old patterns of thinking and feeling usually reappear. The sense of separation reappears but since the peace and happiness of Nirvikalpa samadhi, of our true nature, still lingers, a very deep desire to go back to Nirvikalpa samadhi accompanies the reappearance of the world. For a while we want to reproduce this peace, until it is pointed out that we are still in a dualistic, separating perspective, since we are making the distinction between nirvana, pure consciousness, and samsara, the world.

Then we are asked, "From where does the world arise, where does it abide, and where does it go?" Obviously the answer is, "Consciousness." The answer comes from the experience of Nirvikalpa samadhi. Then we are asked, "If it arises out of consciousness, exists in consciousness, and vanishes back into consciousness, then what is its true nature?" The only possible answer is, "It is consciousness itself." Then we are asked, "Why are you looking for Nirvikalpa samadhi if everything is consciousness? Just stay at rest wherever you are." Then, all of a sudden, we realize that our true nature is always present under all circumstances, that everything is God, that there is nothing that is not God. That is Sahaja samadhi, the natural state.

Sometimes we can clearly see a point of no return, but it is not always like that. However, the deep fear of disappearing, the deep fear of death, doesn't come back. This deep fear is what prevents us from being happy. When it disappears the search becomes a celebration.

What is transmitted by a spiritual friend?

What is really transmitted is the ultimate peace that is present when the fear of disappearing has vanished. This absence of fear communicates itself without your having to make any effort. The words have some interest but they are not the important part.

When a child wakes up frightened of tigers in the middle of the night, it goes into its mother's bedroom and climbs into bed with her. The mother does not need to do anything. She just lies with the child and holds it. Slowly the child's fear dissipates. Why is this? It is because the mother is not afraid of tigers. She is fearless. She doesn't do or transmit anything to the child. However, it is because she is fearless that the child is able to gradually let go of its own fear. The child senses her confidence and her unshakable fearlessness and it is this resonance with its mother's fearlessness that gives it the courage to let go of its own fear. It recognizes her fearlessness as its own.

When the child relates the story the following morning, he may say that his mother comforted him and that it was as a result of this that his fear vanished. However, that is just how that child sees it. The mother knows that she didn't do anything, that it was her fearlessness that was the effective element in the encounter. Everything else was just the packaging that made it possible.

10

Objects Flow Through Us

I felt frustrated this morning because my young son wouldn't settle. I was tangled in a knot of frustration. Then I found myself watching the irritations and frustrations. I suddenly came across a peacefulness, watching the frustration come and go. Later, I heard your words, "Just drop it." At that moment, I didn't know who would do the dropping, what dropping could ever mean, or who the dropper was.

When there is quiet watching, there is nothing to drop. Drop the thought about dropping! There is no dropper. Dropping is the result of understanding. We drop the search when we understand that the search is not going to bring about the happiness that we are looking for. We drop it because it no longer means anything to keep it going.

It is like looking for water in the desert. We dig and dig until somebody points out that there is no water there. Then it suddenly makes sense. "Yes, there is no water; what am I doing?" Often, however, because the habit of digging is so strong, we start digging again until the understanding returns and we stop. At some point, we don't need to run through the story of the man telling us that there is no water, we don't need to go back to this line of reasoning.

We just catch ourselves digging and drop it immediately. It takes less and less time to come to the understanding and after a while, as soon as we catch ourselves digging, it just stops.

There is no dropper of the digging. It is always the same understanding that drops the digging. Nobody drops the digging. It gets dropped. The alleged person is the digger, so he cannot also be the dropper. If there is a dropper of the digger, then the dropper must be the same as the digger. If there is any intention, then this dropping is simply more digging.

In my experience welcoming doesn't happen without an intention and if there is an intention, then it isn't really welcoming, and the thoughts and feelings just crowd in.

When you say that intentional welcoming is not true welcoming, you are formulating an understanding. This understanding itself happened as a result of true welcoming. It is the welcoming of a situation that leads you to the understanding that intentional welcoming is not real welcoming. Since you have this understanding, it is a good tool because whenever you see that there is an intention, by the same token you understand that there is no welcoming. In the light of your understanding, the intention is going to be dropped.

If we judge ourselves, it implies that we would like to be different, that we would like not to have an intention. This means that we have the intention not to have an intention, and this creates one more layer of intention. Don't build up layers of intention. See the mechanism. See that when there is intention, welcoming is prevented. Don't judge it. It's OK. It's part of nature. Intention is natural. Ego is natural. Problems are natural. Absence of problems is also natural. Everything is natural. Everything is OK. Everything is part of the whole picture that is perfect as it is.

Don't judge yourself. There is nobody to be judged. See the intention for what it is. The moment that we see that there is no welcoming, we are already in welcoming. It is only welcoming that enables us to see this situation and this seeing is enough. Trust it. You don't need to do anything about it. Don't create a doer who wants to do something, who wants to improve the welcoming, who is not happy with the way the welcoming is happening or not happening. You have understood that intention is the major obstacle to welcoming. Let this understanding work for you, don't work for it.

I watch perceptions, thoughts, and sensations fade at night. They clearly vanish into me, so the real "I" obviously does not sleep. I resolve to watch the reverse in the morning, but at that time it is not so certain that they come out of me because I seem to wake up in a ready-made world. Can you say more on that?

In the final phase of the world and the body disappearing at night, it accelerates and goes very fast. Then, the same thing happens as they reappear when we wake up. It is very fast. When you were witnessing the sensations fading, there was a double process going on. There was a process at the level of sensation, and at the same time the mind was interpreting like a theoretician trying to match the theory with the experiment. It is important to eliminate the theoretician and to stick to the experiment, to the feeling and the sensation.

The experience of the vanishing of the observer doesn't only happen during this transition from waking to sleeping. When we notice the presence of the observer, we can welcome it completely and watch its disappearance, like watching a sunset. That which remains is our true nature. The observer cannot be aware of this, because the observer is itself perceived. It is a thought, an impersonator, which doesn't observe anything. It is observed.

In my case, when the theoretician became aware that I was awake all the time and that I was the witness of these transitions between states, I realized by the same token that it had actually been like this for years. I just hadn't been able to formulate it at the level of mind nor had the mind been struck by this knowledge, because it goes on beyond the mind.

It happened when I was falling asleep. My physical body dissolved completely, and then there was pure nothingness. This in turn took the shape of the entire dream world. Then I realized that I had been present all the time as this consciousness. Consciousness is like a ball of clay, at one moment taking the shape of the body, then just clay again, and then taking the shape of a dream. The clay itself is pure silence.

The I-feeling is present in the dream. The dream then goes into the clay, and out of the clay, the world of the waking state arises, and the I-feeling arises with it. However, for a long time after this, the feeling of the presence of our true nature remains, so that although the objects of the waking state, including the I-feeling, reappear, they no longer have any hypnotic power over us. This is especially true if we meditate in this way before going off to sleep and, if we do, we find the same state of meditation is present when we wake up.

The "state of meditation" means that objects are present, but we are not hypnotized by them. If we knowingly dehypnotize ourselves from objects when going off to sleep, we find that we are still free from them when we wake up. It does not mean that the objects are not present; it means that we are not stuck to them. This presence often lingers for an hour or so, but if we abide in it knowingly, it remains for the entire day and also as we fall asleep. In this case, it is permanent. The more we abide in it, the more it is felt. In our meetings we cultivate this knowingness and, at some point, we feel it. If there is a pure intention to know it, we will feel it.

Is the observer the same as the I-thought?

Yes, it is the thought that limits what we are to a specific entity that has the capacity to observe. The ego is created by the desire to observe. In fact, it is the desire to observe.

Is it better to be in the I-feeling than to follow the desire?

The pure I-feeling cannot maintain itself. It can go either of two ways: it can either merge with consciousness or it can grow an attribute such as, "I want this," "I am this," "I am happy," "I am not happy," "I am angry," "I am a man." It cannot stay as pure "I." Either it dies and goes back to its source, thus revealing consciousness or, in order to perpetuate itself, it gets busy identifying itself with objects, thereby limiting itself.

Look at your own thoughts and feelings. You can either go back to the I-thought around which they hinge and from here you will be led to its source, which is this welcoming space of consciousness or, if this space is deemed insufficient, the I-thought will arise again and generate agitation, desires, and attributes.

If we go from a thought or feeling back to the "I" around which they revolve, how do we go upstream to the source from there?

This "I" is a perceived thought or feeling. It is perceived by or appears in me, whatever that is, in consciousness. So are we the I-thought or I-feeling, or the consciousness in which it appears? Obviously we are the consciousness in which it appears. Having understood this, we now have the choice either to remain knowingly as this space in which the I-thought or the I-feeling appears or as an object, the "I."

To begin with, as we abide knowingly as this welcoming space, we will find ourselves being dragged back to the thought or feeling of being a limited "I," out of habit. However, the more often we gently return to this welcoming space and remain there in open unknowing, the more natural and easy it will become to remain there, to remain *as* it.

This space of welcoming is always in the now, it *is* the now, and in it all these contractions are revealed. The contractions are avoidance, avoidance of the now, which from the mind's point of view, is boring because there is nothing for it to do there. In fact, the mind does not exist there. It mistakenly construes this silent, luminous space of awareness as nothingness and therefore starts to manufacture desires and fears again.

149

However, there is no need to take the I-thought again and again; it becomes boring if we do. We take the I-thought once and it leads us to this welcoming presence which we are. Then, we remain in this presence, in the now, and face all the contractions, the avoidance, the attraction, the repulsion, the stuff. Gradually, as we face this stuff as it comes up, it loses its connection with the "I" which, no longer identified with an object, merges with the source and is realized as consciousness. To begin with, it seems like an effort to keep returning to the welcoming presence, but at some point it is so natural that it seems to require an effort to leave it. It feels like home. We no longer feel that we need to be entertained.

Would you say that it is more important to let the "I" go in the course of our daily lives or in meditation?

There is no difference. Meditation should be part of daily life and daily life should be meditation. We can put time aside to meditate if we are invited, if it comes out of the desire to cooperate, if it comes from goodwill. However, don't separate it from daily life. Don't feel, "I have done my chores," and then disconnect. If we meditate in the morning and the evening, we will have spontaneous reminders during the day, although we may not recognize them. The moment in which a reminder comes to us is very creative. We just live with it, let it flow through us. Sometimes it is a thought, thinking about the truth. Sometimes it is more like a feeling, being invited by meditation.

If we make a special time for meditation, in order to go towards a goal, then there is some rigidity, some discipline. If we make time for it out of love, without a goal, without the notion that it will take us nearer the mark, that is fine. In the beginning, we may choose to meditate in a certain position, but later the position becomes irrelevant. At some point it is very difficult to tell when we are meditating and when we are not. That's the whole point. It no longer makes any sense to us to make this kind of distinction.

In the beginning, we think about the truth from time to time. Then a time comes when a thought about the truth automatically comes up during every available moment. Later on, this is replaced spontaneously by silence or perhaps a short thought about the truth followed by silence. By then, whenever we are not available, in other words when we are engaged in activity, meditation is still present. However, we shouldn't feel guilty about it if we don't meditate, we shouldn't make it a means towards a goal. Whenever we are invited, we should just respond naturally like any other process in our life, such as breathing, eating, reading a book, or listening to music.

CB

When I see that I am stuck to my body-mind, this observation releases the stuckness, but I don't feel that I remain in my true nature, that I go all the way.

Just go as far as you can. What is essential is our goodwill to go all the way no matter what. If we have this goodwill, then for all practical purposes, it is as good as if we had gone all the way. Some people expect a big event in which they are going to go all the way and be liberated. The solution is much simpler: just be ready to go all the way from moment to moment. That is it. That accomplishes the same thing. That is exactly the position in which one who has gone all the way finds himself or herself. If there is a stain on this willingness, an obstacle, a reluctance, then we have to take a look at it, but for all practical purposes, it is sufficient to be willing to go all the way from moment to moment. To go all the way is not death but a beautiful birth.

There is a longing in the feeling, so it is not quite comfortable.

What does it mean to go all the way? It means complete surrender. Therefore, if there is discomfort, it is no big deal because, if we are ready to go all the way, ready to die for this, a little discomfort is nothing. If we take this point of view, which is the same as welcoming, then providing the welcoming is pure and total, the problem vanishes.

Could you say something about being unfocused? I feel that I should be wider and unfocused, but there is a habit of concentrating on things.

Don't see this ability to concentrate as a drawback. See it as a force in yourself, as an asset. Simply concentrate on being unfocused. This will happen naturally when you understand that the mind will never know what you are, that you will never know in the same way that you know a chair, for instance. However, you will be it.

The same quality of the mind that enables us to focus on an object also enables us to be totally unfocused. People who stand on the path of knowledge, of understanding, usually have the ability to focus on thought. We spontaneously focus on the thought about the truth or the arguments that are expounded here, and this thought about the truth dissolves and leaves us in freedom, leaves us complete. We have nowhere to go. The mind has nowhere to look.

There are two ways of being one-pointed: artificial and natural. The artificial way is the result of effort and practice, just as when we learn to play tennis, we learn to keep our eye on the ball. After years of practice, we are able to do that and at some point, it becomes spontaneous. The other way is through grace. It is the way in which we are focused in love. If we are in love and we finish an activity, we think of our lover. It doesn't require any effort. We fall in love with truth and truth falls in love with us and reminds us of itself whenever we are available. When the thought about truth comes to us spontaneously in this way, we know that it is the effortless way of being one-pointed. We become more and more one-pointed, and it grows effortlessly and naturally. Someone who is in love with truth doesn't need to make an effort to think about truth.

Was there a point in your life when you weren't in love with truth and then one day you were?

Yes. One day I wasn't aware that I was in love with truth, and the next day I was. There was a day before I was in love with truth, and the next day I thought, "Gee! I didn't know truth was so beautiful. I didn't know that it was beyond my wildest dreams!"

Can falling in love with a man or a woman be a steppingstone towards ultimate enlightenment?

It can be a steppingstone and it can also be the stone that makes us fall. When we are in love with a man or woman, we have to see that we are in love with consciousness in that man or woman. In other words, we are in love with the true essence of that man or woman, which is also our own essence.

If we are in love with a beautiful body, we are, whether we know it or not, really in love with beauty itself, towards which this beautiful body points. If we are in love with beautiful qualities, such as intelligence or sensitivity, then we are truly in love with supreme intelligence, receptivity, ultimate consciousness. Sensitivity points towards liveliness, consciousness, life. It is that with which we are in love. Through the apparently limited individual shape, both gross and subtle, we are in love with the essence. In a relationship, the experience of the object sends us back to the essence. In this way, it remains alive. That is possible only if our partner also shares this love knowingly.

We need this deep communication in a relationship, and this is only possible if there is true love. This love in our partner may not be specifically revealed as love for the truth, for the ultimate, but it has to be there and in time, it will reveal itself. Otherwise, we may still be in love with a beautiful form or some beautiful characteristics and, as a result, if we do not have this deep communion, there will be no way we can find a place in which conflicts and oppositions can be resolved.

153

The true function of relationships is the same as the function of anything else in this manifestation. It is to take us to the truth, to grow in understanding, love, and beauty, and to celebrate this. Relationships are perfectly designed to provide continual opportunities to lead us towards truth. They are also perfectly designed to celebrate this understanding, love, and beauty, just as in music, it is good to play duets, trios, and symphonies as well as to play solo. Therefore, if there are difficulties in a relationship, take these difficulties as your yoga exercises. They are very effective! If there are no difficulties, then just celebrate happiness.

ೞ

I am confused about karma and reincarnation and wonder who there is to be reincarnated?

That's a good question! Ask those who believe in reincarnation. I have no view, which means I can have all views. It's fun! You have put it in a nutshell. Who is there to reincarnate? It is not our experience that consciousness is in our body. Our experience is that the body and the mind are in consciousness, so what is there to reincarnate? It is obvious that this body cannot reincarnate; it vanishes and is gone forever. If there is another body, it will be a brand new one. Likewise, the alleged mind dies every time a thought, a perception, or a sensation vanishes. Something that vanishes cannot reincarnate. On the other hand, consciousness has never been incarnated. You should ask those who believe in reincarnation what they think.

When people remember events from a life a long time ago, does that mean that their mind has tapped into universal mind?

This so-called past life is created the moment it is thought about, in the same way that when our own past in this lifetime appears, it is always created in the now. If our own past, of which we are allegedly conscious, is an illusion, then our unconscious past, from past lives, is

154

even more so! Therefore, we first have to investigate the reality of our past in this lifetime. The past is always a figment of our imagination. It only appears in the now. Only the now is real.

Our personal past is based on the concept that we have been traveling through time, that we were there ten years ago, then five years ago, then a minute ago, and so on. However, the reality of our experience is that we are always here and now and that time, events, and appearances are traveling through us. Only the now is real and that which comes and goes is only real as long as it is present. We never go anywhere.

We create the so-called external reality as we go along. In fact, it is not external at all but is always within consciousness. We create our past each time we think about it. However, it is not cast in stone forever. We have many pasts. The past changes from moment to moment, just as the future does. One moment, it seems totally unavoidable that a certain thing will happen. Then something comes out of the blue, and things take a totally unexpected direction. The same thing happens to the past. To believe in reincarnation only reinforces bondage, reinforces the belief system that we are personal entities. It is a tragedy to see doctrines of liberation that reinforce this belief.

Some people in the West think that it is better to replace our Christian belief systems with more sophisticated, more awakened belief systems from the East. However, in doing so, we just move from one hole to another. There is nothing spiritual about reincarnation. It is bondage.

Are you saying that I never had the experience of being a boy, that it is just a memory created in the present?

What is being said is that there has never been a boy moving in time, turning into a young man, then into a middle-aged man, and so on. All of these appearances flowed through consciousness. You, as consciousness, have never been a boy, a young adult, or a middle-aged man. These were perceptions and concepts flowing through consciousness. I am not denying that these perceptions and concepts

155

have flowed though consciousness. That is what memory tells us. However, I am denying the fact that the boy grows into an adult. I am denying the objective existence of these events and the objective existence of time. By "objective," I mean independent from consciousness.

From the vantage point of the totality of this timeless presence, there is no time. Consciousness is not in time or space. All the mind can do is reduce consciousness to a point, whereas it is in fact the totality, of which the mind with this universe is just a speck. Since the mind cannot grasp consciousness, it reduces it to nothingness and then becomes frightened of it.

The timelessness of our true nature is frightening to the mind because it says, "There is no room for me there," and it is true! However, it shouldn't be frightening for the mind because, at the same time, one of the possible modes of existence of this extraordinary potential is whatever is going on right here, right now. There is room for the entire universe, all the galaxies, all the stars, and all the times. So there is no lack of space or time. It is just that the mind has no access to this different dimension.

We take ourselves for an object that is conditioned, subjected to time and space. There is no doubt that the body seems to be so, but we have no right to infer from this that consciousness is either located in or subject to time and space.

CԽ

Turn whatever thought, feeling or perception arises, towards its source. Their source is the "I am." It is consciousness, presence. We have this presence in common with every arising object. Its presence is also our presence.

In true welcoming, in true meditation, the arising thought or feeling is not avoided. It is not repressed. It is completely allowed to reveal presence. It is important to understand clearly that the object does not have to disappear for presence to be revealed. Nothing needs to happen with regard to the object.

We can look at a beautiful painting and, at some point, we feel the beauty. In a sense, the painting disappears, but it disappears in a natural way. It vanishes naturally into beauty. We do not make it happen. We do not move away from the painting towards beauty but rather, we let beauty take us. We let the painting speak to us until we understand the message.

In order for this understanding to take place, we need to be detached from the object. If we look at the painting, being specifically interested in what is going on in the painting, who painted it and when, how much it is worth, how long it has been in the museum, who were its previous owners and so on, we cannot see the beauty of the painting. All that stuff stands between us and the beauty. In order to see the beauty of the painting, we have to look at the painting and be interested only in beauty.

It is the same here in this contemplation of whatever arises in the moment. We don't look away from it. We don't manufacture another object. We look at it. We face it. We let the situation speak to us, being only interested in presence. We don't care about anything else. That is what is meant by "turning the mind inwards," "turning a feeling inwards."

We usually do not know how to look at a painting because we do everything so fast. We should have a sofa in front of it and make acquaintance with it in silence. Of course, we have a first impression, a first aesthetic impression, but the aesthetic impression is not necessarily the seeing of the beauty. The seeing of the beauty is much deeper. It has to truly reach the heart, and then a transforming process takes place.

We have to sit in front of the painting for a while and set aside what we know, what we already like or dislike. We have to be in not-knowing, open to new beauty. It is like when we make acquaintance with someone, we should ideally make acquaintance in silence, being open. We let all the feelings and the thoughts that are triggered by the encounter freely unfold in this contemplation, and then at some point, there is a meeting, especially if both parties are open to the meeting.

The painting that we are contemplating in life is not a rectangle limited by a frame. It is the totality of our experience. It has no boundaries either in space or in time. It is the infinite painting. Forget everything you know about the painting. Forget the name of the painter, God or whatever, the past history of the painting, what you like about the painting, what you dislike about the painting. Forget all of that. Just sit on the sofa of consciousness and contemplate the painting, the totality of your experience in this moment. It has no inside, no outside, no frame, no borders. However, it has a title. The title is "Now." In this contemplation, let the painting lose itself in you and lose yourself in the painting.

When a landscape is painted by a great master, we always discover new details. It is ever new. This is even more true of the painting called "Now." If it seems to be the same old painting, it would mean we are not really contemplating the painting; we are contemplating the stuff about the painting, the trivia, the concepts and feelings about the painting, but not the painting itself. The painting itself is always alive, fresh, and new.

11

Meditation Never Starts or Stops

I know that unless I face fear, I can never be free. However, I cannot face it. The thinking process is an escape from it. I feel trapped. Do I have to face it?

The very fact that you speak of it shows that you are aware of it, which in turn suggests that you have already faced it. If you had not faced it at all, you wouldn't have come up with this question. However, by saying that you cannot face your fear, you indicate that you are afraid of facing it.

Yes.

There, you just faced it! Just before you said, "Yes," you faced it. In order to agree, you first had to become aware that you are afraid of facing your fear and, to become aware of it, you had to face it to some extent. You are not asked to face it in its totality right away, right now. Next time, you can go a little deeper.

It is one thing to face it and another thing to act on it. Fear stops me from doing many things. I can face it, but I cannot take the leap.

Do you want to be free of fear or do you want to feel good? In the beginning, it is not going to feel good.

We say, "I feel bad because . . . because . . . because . . ." Would it be possible to just feel bad without the "because"?

Probably.

Yes. That's what I call facing the fear. Just drop the "because." Just feel bad. When fear comes up, it is a feeling in the body; it has a body-like aspect. It is not just in the head. You turn in circles when you start looking for reasons for it in the mind. It is important to welcome the totality of the situation, including the feelings in your body. Just live with the fear or anger or whatever it is, without escaping from it or finding reasons for it. Stay with it, not just with the thoughts, but with the feelings, also. Contemplate all thoughts and feelings as you would a landscape or a painting. Some paintings are not necessarily pleasant, but you can still contemplate them.

I think that you are speaking from a level where you are aware of your true nature, but as long as I think I am a mind and a body, I can't do this. Fear is very real, and the thought process is designed to avoid the fear. The fear is based on me being a mind and body. I can't do this.

That is true. You can't do this as long as you think that you are your mind and your body. However, you don't always think that you are your mind and your body. There is some freedom. When you don't think, "I am my mind and my body," there is room to face your fear. You are only your mind and your body when you think that way. Don't condemn yourself to ignorance by thinking, "I am always my mind and my body." This thought sometimes occurs. That's fine. So what? However, between such thoughts, you are not your mind and your body. You are whatever you are. Ask yourself, "When I am not thinking that I am my mind or my body, then am I my mind or my body?"

160

That question comes from the mind that I believe is there. It is a thought.

When you don't think, where is your mind?

I always think.

When you feel, hear, or perceive, and between thoughts and perceptions, you are not thinking, so you don't think all the time. You heard these words and you said, "I always think," but before speaking, you had to hear so as to understand what you were being told. You are hearing at this moment. In order to hear, you cannot think. You think after and you think before. The attitude you have when you are hearing these words is not thinking. It is hearing. It is openness. You can develop this attitude and stay open even when no one is speaking.

How is that done?

First, become aware of these moments when you are not thinking. There are many moments when you are open, when you are listening, sensing, or perceiving. Once you have recognized those moments, you won't think of yourself as being continually under the spell of thinking. You will eliminate this false belief, for it is simply a belief. It is not your experience. Then you will discover and become increasingly acquainted with these moments when you are just present, present to yourself, present to whatever is appearing or not appearing. Simply be open.

These moments are free from fear. During such moments, we have to make sure that our openness is complete, that we are not only open intellectually but at all levels, at the level of sensing, feeling the body, and perceiving. In the beginning, it is frightening because it is like letting go of all kinds of pseudo-securing objects, letting go of our foundation somehow. It is like being up in the air without the support of objects.

161

However, we soon get used to it and later, we discover that it is the free state. Further on, we discover that it is a happy state and at some point, we also discover that it is our natural state. In other words, when we are this openness, we are making no effort, we are just as we are, we are just what we are.

Cઠ

I would like to ask about awareness, consciousness. It is said that meditation starts when we stop doing, when we are just being aware, but that is happening anyway.

Meditation never starts or stops. It is our true nature.

So there is awareness present all the time and we just have to see that, rest in that, allow that, and then that develops and just carries on?

Yes. When we see that, a transformation takes place in the body-mind. The body-mind is struck by causeless joy and is set free from the belief that it has to work towards the acquisition of happiness. This happiness is not something that can be reached through effort, through suffering. How could we reach happiness through suffering? How could more suffering make us happy? We have to start from happiness. So often we have accepted more suffering in order to become happy.

There is really no point in trying to understand awareness or consciousness. Is it best to just rest in that awareness, which is already present?

When the understanding is correct, there is no question of trying to rest in what you already are. As long as there is effort, the understanding is not correct. As long as the understanding is not correct, it is normal for the mind to try to understand. The mind will keep running until it reaches a natural stop or rest.

162

Until it realizes that it doesn't have to do anything?

Yes. Not only that it doesn't have to do anything, but also that whatever it does is actually counterproductive. It would be enough to truly understand that. Until that moment, it is useful for the mind to think. In this way a cleansing process, higher reasoning, takes place in the mind. It eliminates the old belief systems including, in the end, the belief system of self-realization.

Presumably, that process will distance emotional problems.

The process of higher reasoning has nothing to do with emotional problems. One has to approach the truth by inquiring in the same way as a scientist approaches scientific truth. He might be in poor health, but once he is sitting in front of his blackboard, all of that disappears. Dispassionate thinking is a precondition for higher reasoning.

That is the opposite of the way I normally think, which is that the circumstances have to be right before I can stop trying, before I can have any peace.

In the direct path that we are talking about here, we go directly to truth, and with this understanding we deal with the problems in our daily life. As we start dealing with these problems from this uninvolved or impersonal perspective, we gradually find that they were all false problems and they will all eventually find harmonious resolutions.

That seems one step removed from where I am. I am still attached. There seems a personal element in my life.

Not necessarily. Put this attachment and personal element in brackets, so to speak, and go directly to the question, "What am I?" Stay there for as long as the personal problems in your life give you the freedom to do so. At such a moment, take into consideration what is being suggested here, that you are the awareness, the consciousness that is understanding these words right this moment, and that this very consciousness is not personal, that we are all the same consciousness.

That is the only thing that needs to be taken into consideration. Doubts will arise in your mind, and you can revisit this issue until the mind is fully convinced. You can re-examine your doubts in the light of what has been suggested here, until your conviction is strong enough to give you the courage to act in accordance with what you have understood. That is the second step.

We have to realize that this consciousness is not personal. In order to realize this, we have to take the first step, which involves coming to the understanding that we are not the body or the mind, but rather the consciousness that perceives both the body and the mind. The second step is to find out, based upon our experience, whether this consciousness is personal or not. This question has to be investigated thoroughly. If the answer is, "No" or, "I don't know," which amounts to the same thing, then from that moment onwards, we are genuinely open to the possibility that this consciousness is universal. We are open to the possibility that it is the trunk of which we as individuals are the branches or the flowers. From that moment onwards, we are prepared to test out this possibility in real-life situations. It is the testing of this possibility in real-life situations that gives us the final answer to the question, "Is consciousness personal or not?" The moment we have the true answer to that question, then all our problems are resolved, because we are no longer a psychological entity, and as such, we don't have psychological problems.

What do you mean by testing it in real-life situations?

In your relationships, for instance, when you are facing a so-called other, it means being open to the possibility that the consciousness behind those eyes in front of you, is the same consciousness that you feel inside yourself. It means being constantly open to the possibility that we are like two flowers looking at each other from two different branches of the same tree, so that if we were to go deep enough inside to the trunk, we would realize that we are one. Just being open to this possibility will have a profound effect on your relationships and on your experience of the world. The result of this experiment comes as an experience, not as a concept, although it may subsequently be formulated by the mind if necessary.

It seems a lot easier when there is no relationship.

That is not true. It is a big mistake. How can we discover that we share consciousness with others if there are no so-called others present to test it? We can go to the Himalayas and live in a cave, and after thirty years there, we can share our consciousness with the snakes. However, it is easier to share it with our neighbor or with a stranger. They are better designed for that purpose. Not only will they help us to discover that consciousness is universal and impersonal, but they are also perfectly designed to share and celebrate this understanding.

∞

I am trying to understand timelessness, eternal presence.

Time is a concept. It is understood as the interval between two events. However, these two events never coexist. When one is present, the other is not, so the other event is non-existent. Time, therefore, is the distance between an existing event, in the now, and a past or a future event that is non-existent. It is like the distance between this point and a unicorn. Therefore, time exists only as a concept. This concept itself appears in the timelessness of consciousness. Identifying the concept with its background, consciousness, creates the illusion of time.

When duration is purified from concepts, it becomes what it has always been, timeless awareness, timeless presence. From the vantage point of this timeless presence, objects flow through it creating the appearance of time. The changes in an object point towards the presence of a changeless witness, for you cannot notice changes without a reference that is changeless. For example, you cannot be aware of motion without something that is motionless.

165

It is like watching a film. In the drama, thirty years may pass, but for the viewer sitting in his chair, it lasts only an hour. The time in the story and the time in the chair are different because we are talking about two different worlds. Similarly, the time in this waking dream seems to exist, but from the vantage point of the witnessing consciousness, sitting on its comfortable chair, the time is always now, presence.

This timelessness is not something unknown to us. It is what we call the "now." The spaciousness in which everything occurs, the eternal now, is this timelessness. We get confused when we try to introduce divisions between past and future within it. Then we forget that we are always at home, always in this now, *as* this now, that there is nothing past or future. We recreate them at every moment.

We have divided our experience into that which is subjective and psychological, and that which is objective or worldly. Subjective time seems to vary. For example, it seems to shrink if we are enjoying ourselves. However, objective time is deemed to be real and stable. We decide that the material world is real and chronological time becomes correspondingly real, as a result. From the vantage point of consciousness, both the subjective, psychological world and the objective world are dreamlike; they are illusions, and so both times are equally illusory.

So do all physical laws just reflect the way that the mind works, rather than accurately describing something that exists objectively?

The laws of physics are the laws that apply to this waking dream. During night dreams, the laws of physics are different. That is why you can fly at night! The laws of causation, which are more general than the laws of physics, apply to both domains. However, at the level of consciousness, there is no causation because there are no objects, there is no duality. At this level, there is one single law, and that is the law of love. At this level, love is the ultimate cause of everything, and it is for this reason that there is no answer to the question, "Why?" Everything is just the playfulness of God showing up at every moment.

166

This body is old and tired.

This body seems to appear in time. In a dream, ten years may pass by in one minute. You may have a baby and then be taking it, as a child, to school. When you wake up, you see that the body in the dream was an illusion, and the time to which it was subjected was also an illusion, but from the vantage point of the dream, it seemed to be real.

We should be open to the possibility that *this* is a dream and when we do, everything changes dramatically. It actually turns out to be so. If this waking experience is seen to be a dream, then our behavior changes and we will find that the response coming from the characters or the situations in this dream also changes.

I have a concept that this body will die.

That seems like a good concept! The true question is, "Am *I* going to die? Who am *I*?" "When the body dies, will *I* die?" That is why the question, "What am I?" is crucial. Do you cry when a shirt becomes too old and you throw it away? No, because it is obvious that you are not the shirt.

You mentioned the recognition of impersonal consciousness. Is that the final effort that an individual can make?

It would be the last effort that an individual would seem to make.

୪

It is said that there is no free will, that no one has any choice.

It is obvious that you have no free will as a person. Ask yourself, when a thought comes to you, whether or not you chose it. Obviously not; otherwise, you would always choose happy thoughts, beautiful thoughts! You don't choose your thoughts. They just appear like clouds. Similarly, when you make a decision, the decision comes as a thought. Therefore, you do not make your decisions.

Everything is an act of God; that is, it comes to you spontaneously out of consciousness, without your having willed or created it as a person. Everything is innocent, God's innocence. If I feel I am a person, then I project a person onto the other so-called individual and judge him guilty. However, no one is guilty because God has done everything. She designed Adam, Eve, the garden, the tree, the apple, and the snake! If you let God take responsibility for it, she will take responsibility beautifully. Do not feel that you are responsible or guilty. Guilt makes us miserable and therefore makes everyone around us miserable.

True responsibility is the sense of happiness that wants to be shared with others. Fathers and mothers take care of their children because they want to share their happiness with them. This responsibility is spontaneous, it comes in the now, from happiness. Guilt comes from the past, from a pseudo-personal entity who allegedly had free will but who actually never existed.

If we do not choose our thoughts, there cannot be a sin or a sinner, because the alleged sinner is the chooser of the sinful thought. However, since the thought is not chosen, there is no chooser and therefore no sinner. There is no personal entity. There never is, in the now. It always comes after the fact as an afterthought, "*I* decided this. *I* did this. It was bad."

Where does discrimination come in? A thought appears, but we don't have to follow that thought. We have the choice.

A thought appears and then a second thought follows, such as, "I am not going to pursue that thought," or, "I am going to pursue that thought." However, these are just thoughts like the first one, and we don't choose this second thought any more than we did the first. There is no choice as an individual, as a personal entity.

The personal body-mind organism has been conditioned and chosen by genetic, environmental, and social programming, as well as by parents, educators, events, and so on. It is a conditioned reaction response to the stimuli received from the surroundings. To try and analyze a body-mind as an isolated psychosomatic system

168

doesn't make sense, because in order to analyze this system, we need to know the condition of the rest of the universe and its laws, of which it is an integral part. It is only then that we could try to predict the outcome of certain events. We cannot therefore locate an isolated individual, even from the materialistic perspective.

Does effort come in or is it all predestined?

The appearance of effort, of a personal doer, can come in, but you can take it deeper by asking, "Why did I come here?" or, "Why am I interested in these questions? Is that predestination?" Although it seems that we came here out of our own volition, it depends on what we call "I." If by "I," we mean a personal identity, a body-mind, then there is no choice. However, if by "I," we mean consciousness, then at that level there is total freedom, because this consciousness is not personal. It is God's consciousness. It is a totality. It is this consciousness that chooses to become interested in itself.

How do you make the distinction between these two inwardly?

True consciousness is the subject. It is the perceiving agent, whereas everything that is personal is perceived. That which perceives, that which is understanding these words, is consciousness. Consciousness can never be seen. If it were seen or felt, it would be an object. It knows itself by itself. If asked whether or not there is consciousness right this moment, you would say, "Yes," without a doubt. That conviction comes from an actual experience. You wouldn't say, "Yes, there is consciousness because my parents said so." You would say that it comes from your own experience, which it is beyond doubt. If then asked to describe the experience from which you derive this answer, you cannot, because it is not an objective experience, and you can only describe objects.

Is it the sense of doership that sometimes makes it difficult to discriminate?

Yes, the sense of doership is associated with this body-mind organism. The sense of doership is fine if it is God's doership, if it is consciousness' doership. Consciousness is the ultimate doer. It creates everything at every moment, and that could be construed as a doing. It even creates the appearance of a doer, of a doing, and of a deed. It is like a theatrical play where there is the appearance of someone killing another person, but in fact there is no murderer, no victim, and no murder. The true creator in that case is the playwright. Consciousness is the playwright.

Everything appears out of this ocean of consciousness. We are not aware of the ocean as an object, but the ocean is aware of itself. When we use the I-thought referring to ourselves, we can say, "I have the flu," in which case, "I" refers to our body. Or we can say, "I am happy," referring to the mind or, "I am conscious," referring to consciousness. The pronoun "I" can be used in many situations. It is important that when we use it, we know clearly to what we are referring. Therefore, we can indulge this use of "I" as long as we know that the true referent is consciousness and that this consciousness is not personal.

Do you know it by feelings or is it beyond that?

The consciousness that knows your feelings and the consciousness that knows mine, is one and the same. However, *it* is not a feeling. If it were a feeling, it would have to be known by something else. It knows itself by itself, but this knowledge cannot be grasped as an object.

Is the "I" not the result of assessing yourself and keeping the boundaries? In order to grow and protect myself, I surely need to be "me."

Just take the I-thought or the I-feeling very deeply. When we want to understand something, we should be open. We shouldn't stick to what we know because if we do, we will not be open to understanding anything new. Either we are happy with the situation, there are no

170

questions, and we don't want to change anything, or we are dissatisfied with our condition, which means that we want to change it. If we want to change it, it implies that there is something that we are thinking or doing that is generating misery, so we have to be open to the new, we have to be open to the possibility of change. Investigate who or what you are in this openness, without knowing, without coming up with answers, without defining yourself. Whenever you come up with an answer, question it.

For instance, ask yourself, "Is it true that I am a woman? Is it true that I am this body? Or am I that consciousness, whatever that is, in which this body, this womanhood appears? What are these words appearing in right this moment? Is it not what we refer to as 'I'? What am I truly? Am I that which is conscious or that *of which* I am conscious? I am conscious of the woman, I am conscious of the body. Therefore, there is something, whatever that is, that is called 'I,' which is conscious of the woman, which was conscious of the baby, and which was conscious of the little girl. What is this 'I'? Is it not me? If it is me, what is its relation with the woman, with the little girl?"

It is for you to see what the truth is. Only your experience, your own openness, your own investigation, and your own freedom with respect to everything that anyone has told you in the past, will let you know. Only you can know who you are, nobody else, not your parents, educators, scientific community, doctors, only you. It is your job.

CЗ

When you say that your thoughts are coming from this ocean, it seems so impersonal. Are you like that all the time?

The ocean in its depth doesn't care about the storm. Everything is possible in this ocean. This ocean is not personal. When you said, "You," you personalized this ocean. You were speaking to a body-mind. A body-mind is just an appearance in this ocean. It has no reality in itself. The ocean is peace itself. You are it. I am it. We all are it.

It is how I would like to live, but it seems impossible.

From the vantage point of a personal entity there is no peace, so from that point of view it *is* impossible. The only way is to understand that you are already this eternal peace. That is the true you. Then these questions won't arise. When this is understood, the chances are that the body-mind will be at peace, but it doesn't matter. You are at peace. You *are* peace.

The whole world is seeking fulfillment.

That which is fulfilled is fulfillment itself. You are that. Find this fulfillment in yourself, as you are. Remain still and then this fulfillment will find you.

If I just notice that the fulfillment is already there, there is nothing to do.

Yes, the doing, the activity, and the misery, veil the happiness that is inherent in our true nature, just as the waves on the ocean seem to eliminate the transparency and the peace of the ocean. When the mind goes quiet, this peace reveals itself. It is causeless. It is not produced.

Do spiritual practices, meditation, self-inquiry, and chanting cause the waves or still them?

They are all part of the doing. However, it depends also on what the ultimate goal is. If the ultimate goal is personal, then it is not true spiritual practice. The best result of such a practice is to bring you to that understanding. However, if the ultimate goal is to find God, to find happiness, which is neither personal nor achieved by the person, then it is sacred practice. In fact, in this case, it already comes from the divine. There are many paths that lead to the same center. At some point, all paths become one, in silence.

Is not life also a teaching process in which we have to choose? Is Hitler an act of God? Is nobody responsible?

Nobody, nobody, nobody! You do not choose your thoughts or your actions as a person and neither does anybody else, because there are no personal entities endowed with free will. The person is chosen; it does not choose. Why not see Hitler as cancer? Cancer has killed many more people than Hitler. We feel that cancer is natural and that Hitler is not. Everything is natural. Everything appears in nature. Hitlers are natural. Although we have these feelings about Hitler, we also know deep inside that the reason that Hitler was the way he was, is because he judged people. From the vantage point of Hitler, there were good people, the Aryans, and bad people, the Jews, the gypsies. Hitler was the way he was because he judged good and bad. The last thing we want to do is become a Hitler ourselves, so don't judge anyone, Hitler included.

So should the likes of Hitler just be left alone to do their thing?

Certainly not. In every situation, we welcome the totality of that situation, including our own responses and reactions. Having looked at the situation with this impartial attitude, we act accordingly, taking everything into consideration. It is the lack of judgment in such a case that enables us to act in the best possible way for all concerned. Judgment comes from an apparent separate entity and is directed towards a similar separate entity. However, discrimination is impersonal and impartial. It comes directly from higher reasoning, from consciousness. It is not mediated through the thought or the feeling "I" as a separate entity. It sees the situation clearly and acts appropriately with efficiency, confidence, and courage.

Peaceful means are employed whenever possible, but varying degrees of force are occasionally necessary. Even apparently violent action may, on very rare occasions, be necessary. However, in this situation, the action taken will come from love of the truth and not from hatred of an individual. Consciousness is spontaneous. It doesn't rely on ready-made solutions. It does whatever is necessary to restore the truth in the situation and is then open for the next moment, without any residue from the past. It is fearless.

I think I recognize the impersonal consciousness, and it feels very limited.

When we have the experience of universal consciousness, no fear remains. It is immediately removed by this insight. It is very easy to find for oneself the answer to the question, "Have I had the experience of impersonal consciousness?" It is the same as the question, "Do I still feel the fear of disappearing?"

Krishnamurti talks of a special insight when listening to an enlightened person. Does this transformation only happen in the mind or is it related to the body as well?

It could go through the mind, through feeling, or through the body. Ultimately, it comes from nowhere. It comes from silence, which is beyond the mind and the body. We could ask a question and the answer, which comes from truth, can reach its destination on the spot, and we say, "Ah, yes," and there is an impersonal glimpse of truth. Or the answer can be received and the understanding dawns later. Or it can happen without even using the intellect. Someone can come and sit here, and realize later that something has changed without their noticing it. They notice that there is more peace, more freedom and, at some point, there is joy, peace, or freedom that knows itself. Causeless means that you cannot pinpoint any object that could be its origin.

174

12

Love in Search of Itself

What are the ways of resting in awareness?

To be knowingly invited by silence. To think about silence, which means to be invited by the thought or question about silence, awareness, or God. To see everything as God. To feel God's presence inside, to think of God, or to perceive everything outside as being God. These are the ways of resting in awareness.

By God, do you mean awareness, consciousness?

Yes. Everything you feel is God. Everything you think is God. Everything you perceive is God.

Do you mean just being aware of what is?

It depends what you mean by being aware. We are aware of objects, that is, thoughts, feelings, and perceptions, but not all of us are aware of being aware. We have to be aware of being aware, of being awareness. Normally, when we are aware of objects, we are completely identified with the object. In India, they call this Savikalpa samadhi, absorption in the object.

175

In such a moment, it seems that our entire experience comprises whatever object is present, be it a thought, feeling, or perception. At some point, we understand that in order to have this experience, something must be present to experience it, to register it, something that is conscious, aware, knowing. We formulate this by saying that our experience comprises that which is conscious and an object. Initially, the object part of the experience seems to be by far the largest part of this experience, and that which is conscious or aware of it, whatever that is, seems small, almost insignificant, but nevertheless we know that it is there. However, as we become more interested in what this conscious presence is, the more significant and tangible it becomes and, by comparison, the more the object diminishes in importance and solidity.

At some point, we realize that it is in fact this conscious presence that is the most stable and lasting element of our experience and that the object itself is, by comparison, fleeting and insubstantial. This process culminates temporarily when we become completely absorbed in this presence. Awareness is aware of itself without an object. This is called Nirvikalpa samadhi, samadhi without objects, absorption in the Self without objects.

When objects reappear, we have the choice of identifying with them again or of remaining aware of awareness in the presence of objects. In this case, the objects themselves are experienced as none other than awareness or God itself, and this is called Sahaja samadhi, the natural state.

These are the three modalities of being aware. The first is ignorance, the second is knowledge of Self in the absence of objects, and the third is knowledge of Self in the presence or absence of objects. The second stage is already a stage of Self-realization, but it doesn't bring about complete happiness because in the presence of objects there might still be some nostalgia for the objectless state. There might still be a desire to go back to pure awareness without an object. At this stage, there can still be a hidden refusal of the present moment, the current situation, so happiness is not established. It is only when we see everything as God that there is stability.

So I have to allow that to happen, be aware of that happening and do nothing else?

We cannot make awareness happen. We have to understand first that we are awareness and not the body-mind, that we are this limitless, infinite, timeless presence. We take our stand in the reality of awareness, not in the illusion of a body-mind organism. Then when objects, appearances, phenomena, reappear, we realize that they arise out of our presence, abide in our presence during their existence, and then vanish back into our presence when they disappear. Their true substance is therefore our very presence.

Once that is understood, at first intellectually, we can welcome every object, every appearance, as being consciousness itself, at least potentially. Then all we have to do is to let it unfold freely until it reveals itself as such. It is a game of hide-and-seek. It requires patience. It requires the knowledge that it is a game and this requires giving objects the room to unfold freely, not manipulating the situation or the objects. Then each situation is like a piece of music and we have to wait for the keynote at the end for the resolution. That is when we receive the beauty of the piece. Before that, there can be dissonance, ugliness, but this ugliness makes us long for the final resolution and then it is beautiful. If it is always harmonious, it is boring! The divine harmony encompasses the totality. You cannot take a piece of Bach and say, "I only like the consonance and not the dissonance." We have to embrace it all. The beauty involves the inclusion of everything.

I am so distracted by objects in meditation.

As a result of the purity of our intention, we are not really interested in the objects that arise during meditation, but rather in the unknown presence in which they arise. We have an inkling of the presence at the precise moment that an object arises and again when an object vanishes, if the intention is directed towards the presence, not towards the object.

The difficulty is that we may try to create an absence in the mind, a blank space, which would impersonate the presence. However, all that needs to be done is to make sure that the intention, the sacred intention, is there in the background and to trust it.

The mind will no longer feel it has to create the pseudo presence. As a result, the real presence takes over because it has always been there effortlessly. The fact that the mind does not see the presence, does not mean that it is not there. The mind cannot see the consciousness that is understanding these words in this very moment. This consciousness is not a thought or a feeling. We are it, without making an effort to be it. We have always been this consciousness, this presence. What we are not, appears in it and disappears in it. Because everything appears in it and disappears in it, this consciousness itself has no boundaries. Boundaries appear and disappear like everything else. Consciousness shines between the appearances of the objects and during the presence of the objects. In fact it shines *as* these objects.

In meditation, we take our attention away from all objects, from all appearances. Don't try to transform whatever appears. It is our very intention to change things that perpetuate them. Let everything blossom in presence. Surrender all appearances to this presence. Let this presence create them, maintain them, and allow them to disappear.

At every moment, everything is suspended in God's invisible arms. Everything is free-floating in presence. This presence is everywhere and therefore we are not excluded. It is this very presence that permeates the mind, the body, and the world, as consciousness.

Surrender your mind, everything you think you know, everything you want, everything you have, to this presence. Be in innocence and in not knowing, in "childlikeness." Don't be afraid of letting go of your concepts. They are not your life. There is a life beyond concepts. There is eternal life beyond the me-concept.

178

In meditation, our intention is with the consciousness that lies behind, beyond, and between the objects, whatever objects are being perceived at any moment. That gives total freedom for the objects to evolve, to tell their story, to do their performance, and then salute and leave.

CB

I enjoyed sitting in the park today until some youths came along swearing and totally disrupted the peace. I hated them and in the end I moved. What would have been the enlightened approach?

To move sooner!

There are sometimes more unpleasant situations than pleasant ones, so there has to be some acceptance.

These situations are your yoga exercises. It is very interesting to observe your reactions. The chances are that if you observe and welcome these reactions in yourself, you may still have to move, but these situations will not surface too often. These types of situations arise in order to teach us to be welcoming at all times. There are levels in welcoming and we progress from one level to another. As long as we have not mastered a certain level, the same type of situation will keep on repeating itself until we are able to gracefully accept the situation, knowing that it is God.

I am not suggesting you subject yourself to mistreatment or abuse. There are intelligent ways to welcome the totality of the situation and then move on quietly, without any anger, resentment, or division. There can even be the understanding that it is these people's freedom to behave the way they do and that it is fine if they are having a good time or at least think they are. If we make our happiness dependent upon the way other people behave towards us, we are in trouble.

The same principle applies to accepting and allowing war as well, but it still brings sadness. All the human despair, indignity, ignorance, and lack of compassion. Do you not feel it?

People are tortured by cancer and die in millions. Do you feel it? Suffering touches me but not the lack of compassion. Who am I to judge? The problem is that people kill each other because they judge each other. If I start judging them, I become like them. Why would I do that? I don't see the situation as something that happens to individuals. I see it as a situation that arises in consciousness, like cancer, death, or any other situation. I care about the now, about my neighbor. You think things should be different in order to be happy.

Cancer can be accepted as a natural part of life. Are you saying that the conflict and violence that mankind perpetrates is natural as well?

Yes. It is also a natural disaster that human beings lack compassion. We have to go to the root of this specific natural disaster and ask, "Why?"

It is because most people feel that they are separate entities. At the root of war, at the root of lack of compassion, there is the ego, the notion that I am a separate, personal entity. How am I going to liberate everybody from their ego? Maybe that is not my mission. It is ambitious and pretentious.

All we can do is work on ourselves. We can start with our own sense of being separate, with our own judgment, with our own feeling that things should be different, with our own refusal of the present situation, with our own refusal of others. As a person, we are not going to save the world and perhaps the world doesn't need to be saved. All we can do as a person is to do our best. To do our best, we start by liberating ourselves from our own ignorance. We stop stirring up more disharmony and conflict in the world by freeing ourselves from inner conflict, which comes from fragmentation. In this process we discover our eternity, our immortality. That will fill us up to the brim with happiness, and this will overflow and start resonating in others around us, without our doing anything to cause it. That is the only way to be happy and to do our best in the world as we know it. I am not suggesting that if we have a job in the world

180

that involved helping others, we shouldn't do it. Of course we should. However, it is the understanding that is important, because it is the understanding that is truly implemented in any activity.

It seems that you are speaking of yourself as an individual. If we are consciousness, how do I understand that I am infinite consciousness and also an individual?

You are not an individual at all. That which is overflowing with happiness is happiness itself. It is not the individual that is overflowing with happiness. Light, consciousness, is aware of every individual in the world. It is the same light that is you and I. There are not two lights. The notion of an enlightened person is absurd. The right reason for attending these meetings or reading spiritual books is to resonate with what is said, not to create theories about enlightened body-minds.

How does one come to absolute illumination?

Forget about becoming enlightened.

Is there anything I should do instead?

Nothing! When you are doing nothing, looking for nothing, you are enlightened. You are light, you have always been light. You cannot become what you already are. We are all the same light. As long as you believe that you are an individual there might be a practice, but why stick to the notion that you are an individual? Once you jettison the notion that you are an individual, there is no practice.

If I want to drop the concept and be enlightened . . .

Drop both the concept of being an individual and the concept of being enlightened.

Will I not just get lost in the world without any concept of spirituality?

To be happy is to be spiritual. To be unhappy is not to be spiritual. Don't worry about being happy. Just be happy.

181

If you were enlightened, would you still be on this earth?

I am not on this earth and neither are you. This earth is in you. I am not this body and you are not that body either. The body seems to be on this earth but the body is, in fact, in consciousness. This earth is also in consciousness. The mind, too, is in consciousness. That is the truth of our experience.

Your body is the form that channels this teaching, that relates.

The channel is not important. It is the origin of the message that is important. The message is that the origin of the message is not the channel, that the receiver of the message is not the receiving channel, and that the origin and the receiver of the message are one and the same.

If everything is God's will, then whether we are happy or unhappy is not under our will. Likewise, would we have control over dropping concepts or not?

Your question is based upon the assumption that what you call "we" is a body-mind. If that is so, then what you say is true. However, we are much more than a body-mind. We are consciousness. As consciousness we have freedom. We *are* freedom.

The question of free will sometimes seems unclear because there is a confusion of levels. Once the distinction is made between the level of consciousness and the level of body-mind, everything becomes clear. There is no freedom at the level of the body-mind. There is absolute freedom at the level of consciousness. That which is perceived is not free. That which perceives is freedom itself.

So are happiness or unhappiness, enlightenment or unenlightenment, all in the body-mind realm?

They *are* the body-mind realm. States are irrelevant to consciousness, just as a mirror is completely immune to the images that are reflected in it. They may be pleasant or terrible, but the mirror remains totally unaffected by the reflections. A violent scene reflected in the mirror is not going to destroy the mirror. That is the freedom of the mirror.

The mirror is free from the images. This analogy enables us to understand the freedom of consciousness. Consciousness is the invisible, witnessing presence. It witnesses all states without being affected by any of them in any way.

All things ultimately point towards our presence. All states celebrate our presence. All states have the sole purpose of taking us back to our true nature and then, having recognized it, it is for us to celebrate our eternal freedom.

It feels as though it is something within.

If you are invited by the source, just say, "Yes." Don't ask questions. If you are not invited, that is fine also. Know that the source is still present even when it seems that you are not invited. Don't make a distinction at that moment between a state in which you are invited and a state in which you are not. They are both states. Therefore, they are both reflections within the mirror. Don't worry about states. Know that you are the mirror at all times. There is not one single moment when you are not what you are.

You say that we should just be happy, but it is challenging to be happy all the time.

It is not challenging to be happy. It is challenging to be unhappy. When you say that it is challenging to be happy, it suggests that happiness involves effort, constant vigilance, struggle. If we believe that happiness requires effort and struggle, it only perpetuates misery. Happiness is when we let go and let God. Liberate yourself from the belief that happiness is challenging. Think instead, "Misery is challenging. It requires a constant struggle to fulfill an ego that can never be fulfilled."

That requires vigilance.

Vigilance sounds challenging to me! What about surrender, abandonment? Surrender your fear. Surrender everything you believe. You have to, sooner or later. You cannot take your belief systems with you when you pass away, so why not surrender them now? Surrender your beliefs from moment to moment. Discover the joy of living without attachment to any belief system. The attachment to beliefs such as, "Happiness requires effort," or, "It is necessary to suffer in order to be happy," is very deep.

There are people who join monastic orders, renounce all their possessions, become celibate and give up everything except their notion of God. This notion of God becomes their dearest attachment. Human beings are the most attached creatures. In fact, belief systems are nothing. They are quite easy to let go of. They are just paper tigers! It is better to let them go right now and live happily forever after.

It seems as though the root of this sticky substance that makes bliss come and go is seeking some protection from the fear.

I don't sell fear insurance! When you go on a skiing holiday or buy a Porsche, there is always some danger involved. When you start a relationship with someone, there is potentially big danger! When you eat food, it could be poisonous. Basically, life is dangerous but at the same time it is beautiful, it is interesting. If you travel to an exotic country, it is exciting precisely because it is exotic. There may be inconveniences but there is a thrill about it. Likewise, there is a thrill in this spiritual journey, the thrill of discovering your fear, going beyond it and, on top of that, there is no danger. In fact, it is the only thing in life that is not dangerous. Everything else threatens you at every moment. There is no risk. On the contrary, it will keep you safe! You have got it upside down. It is your current attitude that is dangerous. To take this interesting journey into this exotic land called "fear" is not dangerous.

ॐ

You said that every state, inner and outer . . .

They are all inner, in consciousness.

. . . that every state is a celebration of happiness. However, if I met someone who is harming someone else in front of me, it seems anti-happiness.

Maybe it will touch a place of love in you, of compassion. Out of this compassion, some action will flow.

Is the harmful act itself love?

Yes, if the harmful act was necessary to ignite love and compassion in you. Ultimately, even hostility comes from love.

It hurts me to witness a harmful act.

You want the world to be different. Let us assume that you were given the power to erase the world as it is and reconstruct it as you would like it to be: no wars, no tyrants, no mosquitoes, no cancer, no pain, and everybody smiles. You would end up with something that is very boring, something with no flavor. Then you start adding a bit of salt and pepper and, at the end, you would be back where you started, having realized that it was perfect the way it was!

The only reason that the world seems imperfect is because of death. As long as you believe in the reality of death, the world will be a problem. It will never be perfect. The problem is not suffering or misery, it is the belief that you are a body-mind and are therefore going to die. If you realize that death is not real then, somehow, the world will appear in a totally different light.

This doesn't mean that you are going to go out and kill people, nor does it prevent you from taking part in any action that by common standards would be compassionate, such as finding a cure for cancer. The chances are that most of your behavior would be compassionate, but there will be no inner fear, no inner burden, no inner misery.

185

I am still having trouble imagining how a person actually harming someone else could be a bit of spice in life.

That is because you believe in persons. In order to find the possible explanation for such an event, look at the events that have taken place in your own life. You have been subjected to harm by other people, by nature, illnesses, situations, loved ones having problems. If you think about it, you will see that the outcome of all these events was to take you to the inquiry that you are conducting now, to give you the maturity to investigate your true nature. If you look at things that way, you understand that all events in your own life were necessary to make you grow, to take you closer to happiness. Once you understand that in your own case, you don't have the same judgment about what you see happening around you, because what is true for you is true for all of us.

There are two ways to interpret events. One is at face value, as you have been doing, and this is the perspective of the individual, based upon the existence of personal entities, personal doers. The other way is that there is only one doer, which is God, and that everything is God unfolding. God apparently doing harm to another person is only this movement towards light, towards happiness. It doesn't mean that when facing a situation involving another person, we are going to remain passive. On the contrary, we may take remedial action but, deep inside, we are not affected. It is precisely this which enables us to take the right action, because our interpretation is not colored by the sense of being a separate individual. As a result, we are not angry with the one who is violent because he is in fact also a victim, just like the victim of the violence. They are both learning and we are also learning. There is only learning.

186

If there is no one here, why should there be an individual who has to go through a process of achieving anything?

Ultimately, there is no individual. There is only the appearance of an individual. It is a play. There is no King Lear and no Hamlet in reality but, for the purpose of the play, there is King Lear or Hamlet. We are talking about two different levels and we shouldn't confuse them.

How do I face the fear of death?

Start with any feeling of fear and welcome it completely, without naming it. If a fear comes with a particular association, for example, "I am afraid of elevators," and we inquire into the origin of this fear, we soon realize that the idea of elevators is merely an attribute that is superimposed onto the essential fear. The fear itself stands on its own, independent of any cause. It is a fundamental feeling. This unnamed root fear is the pure fear of disappearance, fear of death.

As we go more profoundly into this welcoming, we realize that this fear is very deeply rooted in the body, and it can reveal itself intensely as panic. It is based on the I-thought and the I-feeling, such as, "I am separate" or, "I don't want to disappear." "I" as a personal entity doesn't exist. Its sole existence is the I-thought or the I-feeling in the body. Apart from thinking and feeling "I," along with all the adjuncts such as, "I am a woman," "I am happy," "I am unhappy," "I am afraid," "I" as a separate entity has no real existence.

We have surrounded ourselves with all these adjuncts and activities in order to perpetuate ignorance, to perpetuate the illusion that we are separate. The moment that we start looking at this bundle of thoughts and feelings, which we call the ego or the person, from an impersonal perspective, just facing it without any attachment, with loving, benevolent curiosity, it starts unfolding. It starts going back to peace, layer after layer, until we reach the ultimate level of fear, the root fear. Then, beyond that, there is the "I," a little thing, a poor thing, the crying child, the basic mistake. This is the mistake from which all other mistakes arise: the identification of consciousness, which is understanding these words

187

right this moment, with a perceived object, with the I-thought or the I-feeling. The mind cannot go to that root because it is itself a perceived object made of thoughts, feelings, and perceptions. The mind is perceived. That which perceives it is beyond it. That is free forever. That is our true nature, our true identity.

I am very lazy. I love the idea that I don't have to do anything, and yet if I don't do anything and just sit at home . . .

Your understanding of "doing nothing" is incomplete. "Doing nothing" doesn't mean not doing anything that your ego dislikes. For instance, "not making any effort" means to understand that thinking in most cases is an effort, that everything, any action, thought, or feeling that comes from the notion that you are separate, is an effort. To stop all effort means to stop all action, thought, or feeling that comes from conflict, from a fragment, from fragmentation. The only way it can be stopped is by understanding that such a thought, activity, or feeling cannot take you to happiness. As long as you have the slightest belief that personal activity can take you to happiness, you will keep generating such activities.

You have to be totally convinced, and then you will find yourself in a state that is very innocent, that could almost be described as a state of stupidity, because when the mind goes silent it feels stupid. However, in this case, the stupidity has been brought about by the highest understanding. You just stay there and from there, magically, you know all you need to know, you receive all you need to receive and you give all you need to give. In this knowing, receiving, and giving, there is great happiness, living from moment to moment in unknowing.

Immense effort that comes from love and that creates suffering may not be personal. Is that all right?

That which comes from love is surrender, not effort. It is the surrender of resistance. It may seem from the vantage point of an external observer that it requires immense effort, but the inner experience is one of flowing with love. When you fly on the wings of love there is no effort. You soar.

188

13

Peace, the Universal Container

Is meditation an activity?

Although in this perspective, meditation is understood as that which we are at all times, it is sometimes referred to, in a more relative sense, as a period of time during which we sit in silence and are present without intention to whatever appears in our awareness. However, it would be wrong to construe this as a practice, as an activity motivated towards a goal. On the contrary, it is the complete lack of any motivation in this experiment that enables us to become aware of the motivated activities of the body and mind, of which we are normally unaware.

All kinds of subliminal efforts and tensions may come to the surface in this silence. However, when these efforts and tensions appear, they are of course felt as our present experience. Therefore, they may fool us into thinking that sitting in silence in this way is actually an effort or a tension that we are doing or creating in that moment. In fact, the opposite is true: we are not making any effort, and it is precisely because of this, that efforts and tensions of which we were previously unaware, come into the light of our awareness.

That is all that needs to happen. If we were to do anything about these efforts and tensions, then that would indeed be an effort! We would be adding another layer of effort.

Is this why it is said that there is nothing to do?

It is true that there is nothing to do but, as a person, we do not have a choice to do or not to do. It is important to understand clearly what is meant by, "There is nothing to do." We have to be careful of thinking that, as a person, there is nothing we can do, because the person is already an activity, a contraction within consciousness. The person is not an entity. It is an activity.

Therefore, to say in this case, "I have nothing to do," betrays the fact that we have not yet understood that we are already doing something. This insistence that there is nothing to do as a person, yet at the same time feeling that one is a person, is one of the subtler ways in which the ego, the activity of thinking and feeling oneself to be person, a separate entity, maintains itself.

Of course, when we understand that the person is a thought or a feeling with no independent volition or capacity for action, then the question of doing or not doing doesn't arise. The person can never do or not do anything, because it is a perceived object. If we think and feel that we are a person, we cannot say at the same time that we are not doing anything. The person is an activity, the activity of thinking and feeling that we are separate, limited entities. It is not an entity. Of course, it is important not to add any further activity to this activity of thinking and feeling that we are a separate entity, and this is what is meant by "not doing." In this case, in our welcoming presence, all these subtle activities of which we were previously unaware will come to the surface layer after layer, and gradually the system will go back to normal.

What do you mean by transparency?

Sometimes during meditation, it is suggested that you make simple movements of the body and, in this case, "transparency" is a term that is used to indicate a movement that is free from volition and resistance. When we want something, we often maintain its opposite. We reject, we resist what is. For instance, if we want something new to happen, it is often because we don't want what is currently happening, so the desire and the resistance are part of the same movement. Wherever there is this sort of volition, there is also resistance. Therefore volition is violent in some way, because it has to overcome this resistance. A motion that doesn't have volition is organic. If we want something and thereby maintain its opposite, there is some waste of energy in this movement. It is not functional. It is not organic.

At the level of feelings, we are aware of the resistance as well as the effort necessary to overcome it. We are so used to feeling resistance and to overcoming it without noticing it, that it feels natural. It is the presence of this resistance that generates a lack of transparency. If, during any activity, we are completely present at every moment, any resistance that we encounter is unable to become established and is therefore dissolved.

It is a gradual process in which the body is purified of tensions, and this in turn dissolves the impression that there is a doer of our movements. The resistance and the effort to overcome it, create the impression of a doer. When the movement is transparent, there is no longer an apparent doer. It is enough to be aware of the resistance without having to get rid of it. In order to become aware of the resistance, it is suggested that you make the movement as transparent as possible.

Is that why, when I leave after doing these movements and start to move, I feel disoriented?

Perhaps. Usually, instead of making the required effort for whatever we have to do, we do more than is necessary. As a result, there is a surplus of effort during the activity and this surplus remains after the activity is completed. This residue of surplus effort creates the impression that there is someone doing it. It is the ego.

191

This is true at many levels. For instance, if a child is doing something that is hard work and no one is watching him, he will do it naturally. However, if somebody is watching him, in order to make it clear that he is making a big effort, he will sometimes act in such a way that everyone notices him. It is this acting that creates the notion of a person. We do it unconsciously. To play any sport well, it is necessary to purify our movements from all kinds of unnecessary effort.

It is important not to allow the notion of a separate entity to remain hidden in our feelings and movements. It should be exposed. If we harbor the belief that to be a separate entity is implicit in the fact that we move and feel the body, it will be very hard to be free of this notion in other areas of our life, such as our thoughts.

Does spontaneous action come from totality?

Yes. Ultimately, all actions come from the totality. Spontaneous action comes directly and knowingly from the totality, whereas unspontaneous action comes from the belief and the feeling that I am a doer, and that I, this doer, exist before, during, and after the action.

A tennis player provides a good example of this resistance. He may love playing tennis in the heat for three hours, against a tough opponent. There may be a lot of effort in the body, but since he loves playing tennis, he enjoys the game. When he goes home, his legs are tired and his wife asks him to take the rubbish out. It is nothing compared to the effort he was making during the game, and yet now there is some resistance!

The body usually gets overlooked during meditation, which is why it is such a good hiding place for the notion of being separate. This notion of being a separate entity is localized in various parts of the body and often remains undetected, although we may be aware of a vague feeling of dissatisfaction.

We do not see these localizations clearly, and so they remain in a twilight zone and fool us into believing that we are these localizations, that we are the body. The analogy of mistaking a rope for a snake is a good example of this. If there is complete darkness, we see neither the rope nor the snake. In full light, we see only the rope. It is only in the twilight that we think we see the snake. Likewise, these incompletely seen feelings in the body create the illusion that there is someone there, and this in turn gives credence to the notion that I am a separate person. They maintain it as an apparent experience. The moment I completely welcome these sensations, it immediately becomes apparent that they are out there, in the open. How then could I possibly be any of those sensations? They are no more or less myself than the song of the birds.

The fact that other perceptions such as sounds and sights often come in familiar patterns, compounds this sense of being a person. For example, when looking at one's face in the mirror, the reflection is almost the same each time. This repetitive pattern makes a convincing case for the existence of a separate entity. So, if I am not an individual, why is it that these experiences have such a common thread?

The fact that a pattern repeats itself does not imply that we are that pattern. Every morning, when we go to the bathroom, roughly the same scene presents itself, the toothbrush, the towel, and so on, but we don't infer from this that we are the bathroom! This repetitiveness creates the notion of a solid object. That is what solid, tangible objects are: highly repetitive patterns. The patterns that appear in dreams have much higher frequencies. They don't last very long and, therefore, don't give rise to the notion of a solid object. They change and evolve very fast, so that the time scale of the night dream is very different from that of the waking dream.

Everything we see is more or less a habit. The body itself is a habit, molecules dancing in a certain way. However, we shouldn't conclude from its repetitiveness that we are this body-dance here and not that toothbrush-dance over there. It is strange, but it is meant to be! Its purpose is to create this extraordinary display of Maya. It is not only strange that I find the same body each morning in the mirror, but it is equally strange that I find the same toothbrush there. The toothbrush exists only when perceived. It is created at the moment of perception, then vanishes into nothingness when it is no longer perceived and is recreated when it is perceived again.

෨

Is there only one viewpoint? There is an inference that there are many.

If we are open to the possibility that the consciousness from which the question comes and the consciousness from which the answer comes is one and the same, then it will turn out to be so. This is a great mystery. The revelation that consciousness is not personal could truly be called enlightenment. If we understand that everything is consciousness, then this consciousness is actually experienced as the substance and substratum of everything we know, feel, or perceive. However, as long as we still believe or feel that this consciousness is personal, we are not knowingly in the realm of consciousness, and what is being mistaken for consciousness is in fact still the personal mind. At that level, we may have understood that everything is mind, but we have not crossed the bridge.

We have to be open to the possibility that we all have this consciousness in common, that we all *are* this same consciousness. We have to be open to this miracle, to this different dimension, which is the dimension of the sacred. If we are open to this dimension, it will somehow enlighten us. The manner in which we become enlightened is up to that dimension, but we need to be convinced. Then, it will show up. In our dialogues, we use reason to understand that there are no logical, valid arguments or facts to substantiate the claim that consciousness is personal. This is as far as we can go with the mind and it leaves us free. It leaves us open. To prove that it is impersonal is beyond reason. It comes from a different dimension. It comes from consciousness itself, from light itself.

We receive glimpse after glimpse of this, until gradually it opens us up completely and the possibility becomes reality. The understanding is that there is only one consciousness here and also there. In fact, consciousness is always here, but this "here" is everywhere.

All that is needed is to be free from old concepts. That is important. To see that they don't have any credibility leaves us in an attitude of not knowing, an attitude in which we have forgotten everything we knew, in which we have nothing. That is the meaning of being "poor in spirit." We know nothing, have nothing, want nothing.

Before initiation in some traditions, one is asked to write a philosophical testament of everything he believes. At initiation this precious testimony gets burnt in front of his eyes. It doesn't matter what it contains; it has no value. It is a symbol of the fact that in order to receive light or understanding, we have to be in freedom, free from beliefs, open.

It seems that the last freedom we are left with is the freedom to choose a thought or not to choose it.

Do you choose your thoughts or do they come to you unchosen?

My experience is that they come and that I choose whether to welcome them or not.

A thought comes to you out of the blue and the next thought that appears is, "Shall I go along with it or not?" However, is it really your experience that you choose this second thought, or does it just come to you as the first one did? In other words, do you choose the thought that chooses? That is the first thing to investigate. When you realize that you are thinking about something, the previous thought has already stopped. The realization that you are thinking is a second thought. It comes to you unchosen.

Is it valid to try to reduce negative thoughts?

It is valid only if we choose our thoughts. If we do not, then what validity can it have? The most important thing is to get rid of the notion that we choose our thoughts. We are control freaks! The moment we realize that we do not control our thoughts, we completely lose control. When I was a child, there were mock steering wheels for cars so that we could sit in the front seat and pretend we were in control. When we realize that we do not control our thoughts, we change seats! It is an important shift. It is liberating to realize that we might as well stop this unnecessary steering and all the thinking that goes with it.

What is a thought?

The thought that arose just before you uttered this question came from silence. So, a thought is silence with a shape. It is made of silence and is a continuation of silence. When the thought is understood, it dissolves again into silence and in doing so, reveals its meaning, but it has remained as silence all the time.

It has been said that if we give attention to certain thoughts, such as negative ones, we strengthen them.

That is true, but not as a person. As a person, we don't choose our thoughts. They just come out of consciousness, out of the source. If we say, "Don't indulge in negative thinking because the more you do, the more it will perpetuate itself," we are not talking to a person. We are talking to that which truly creates thoughts, to consciousness, to that which has the power to produce or not produce thoughts. It would be meaningless to address the thoughts themselves. Thoughts cannot listen nor can they reproduce! The person is a thought or a feeling that appears from time to time in consciousness. It is an object in consciousness that has no power or facility to hear, choose, decide, or to do anything else, for that matter. Therefore, if we say this, we are really talking to consciousness, not to the person. Usually, it is taken personally and is therefore followed by a feeling of powerlessness, because at some level we recognize that as a person, we can do nothing. However, this saying is not directed towards an individual. It is like a prayer that comes from consciousness and is directed towards consciousness.

Can consciousness be conditioned by saying, "Don't do this?"

We are just saying, "Stop doing that!" It is consciousness telling itself, "Stop doing that!" Consciousness hears what it is telling itself to do and it can stop because it has the power to stop. This is the efficacy of prayer.

Does one's own mental activity have the same effect on consciousness?

Nobody owns thoughts. Only consciousness owns thoughts. No private entity owns them.

It seems that for a certain person, the same thoughts keep coming into the space of consciousness.

Yes, at the subtle level, that is what the alleged person is, a certain habitual way of thinking. At the gross level, this person is the so-called body, which is a certain pattern of molecules and cells dancing together.

If what you say is true, then I should be able to change places with you, but I don't think that would work!

It wouldn't work simply because you think it wouldn't work. What makes this perspective seem unlikely is our assumption that consciousness is personal. This complicates everything because, obviously, a personal consciousness could not possibly be that which creates and contains the totality. When we say that everything is contained and suspended in consciousness at every moment, it seems impossible only because we conceive of consciousness as personal. However, if we replace the word "consciousness" by the word "God," it suddenly feels OK.

If we ask why it seems unlikely or impossible when we use the word "consciousness" and yet possible when we use the word "God," we see that it is because we attach the notion of a separate entity to the word "consciousness," we always conceive of it as being personal. However, when we use the word "God," there is the tendency to think of God as being out there, at an infinite distance from where we are, and therefore we lose the sense of intimacy with it. It seems like something beyond our experience.

However, when we talk about consciousness, we evoke this experiential connection with it, because it is our "I am-ness." Perhaps we should use a different word, like "God consciousness" or "divine consciousness." If we take the infinite and universal quality implied by the word "God," together with the intimate and direct connection we feel when the word "consciousness" is used, then we are closer to the truth. It removes the unlikeliness, the impossibility.

ᑣ

I understand that there is nowhere to go and nothing to do, but a kind of laziness has crept in accompanied by a feeling that everything is all right.

Endeavor becomes spiritual the moment it takes us beyond the limitations of a personal entity towards the universal. At that moment we become truth seekers. This desire for absolute freedom comes from freedom itself. However, we are so attached to the belief that we are a personal entity, that we are not yet ready to give credibility to the possibility that we are already the consciousness for which we are looking, and that it is our true nature.

There is apparently someone who wants to liberate himself from bondage and there is an undertaking aimed at doing so. There are many paths that are offered to such spiritual seekers and they all end up at the same point. When we deeply understand that there is no personal entity that is bound, who seeks freedom, or is liberated, then we are in the final stretch. That is the direct path. It doesn't mean that everything we have done before was unnecessary. Every single element of the journey was necessary to take us there, but now there is nothing to do. Once we are there, why worry?

A doubt came in that there was something to do.

The idea that there is something to do always arises from the feeling that things are not right as they are, that they should be different. That is what we have to investigate. This idea always comes from the notion that happiness and peace are dependent on circumstances, so that changing the circumstances would enable us to find them. However, everything that is present now is already present in peace. Peace is the universal container of all things. We do not have to secure peace. It is the stuff of which everything is made. When that is understood we no longer try to change things because we realize the situation is already made of peace. It is pure peace.

Does impersonal consciousness take part in the enjoyment? This morning in meditation a bird sang and it was very clear, very beautiful. Then it sang again, and it was just a sound outside and the appreciation of the beauty had stopped.

It is because this beauty is everywhere, but it is not in the object. The object "bird" only celebrates this beauty. If we look at the bird as a potential container of beauty, we lose it, because next time it is going to appear somewhere else, and again the next time it is going to be nowhere and everywhere. It is a game of hide-and-seek that we are playing with ourselves. What we are is teasing us and is appearing in the most unlikely places because of its universal power to be everywhere. If we believe it is in the birds, it won't be. If we believe it is not in the birds, it shows up there! In this way, it teaches us how to be multi-dimensionally open, without any choosing.

199

If we are fully aware of a thought, we are free of it. If we were fully aware of the concept of being a personal entity, would we not be free? It is as though the separate entity is not fully looked at.

Exactly. It takes place at two levels, the level of thoughts and the level of feelings. At the level of mind, thoughts arise that involve this notion of being separate. The fact that they arise is not a problem at all. The fact that we give them credibility is a problem.

At the level of our body, there are layers and layers of feeling with which we identify. If these feelings are completely welcomed, they lose their power to make us believe that we are these feelings, and we begin to realize that we have always been the welcoming presence in which they arise.

We have to reach the stage when, if asked what we are, no image or sensation could possibly arise to answer the question. We immediately, instinctively feel, "I don't know." This question connects us directly with our most intimate reality, free from all images.

The images I have of myself seem to have such deep roots. It seems almost impossible not to think of myself as something.

Welcome the totality of your experience, without interpretation, judgment, comparison, or conclusion. Just stay with the facts. Let them unfold. Sit quietly and ask yourself if, in the current circumstances, there are still personal thoughts, personal feelings. It is important to understand that sense perceptions, bodily sensations, practical thoughts, creative thoughts, and thoughts about the truth are impersonal. They are not a problem.

What do we do if there are personal thoughts or feelings, such as likes and dislikes or fears and desires, still present? We certainly do not try to eliminate them nor do we try to do what they are asking us to do. We stay on the razor's edge, neither trying to escape them nor eliminate them, nor do we become subservient to them. Looking for the "pleasant" or trying to avoid the "unpleasant" is not the position of one who is in love with truth. Looking for truth regardless of what is pleasant or unpleasant is the position. It is

200

important to see where you stand in your meditation. Are you looking for pleasure, for states, or are you looking for truth? Be clear and honest with yourself.

When you are really looking for truth, all states become neutral: the pleasant ones cease to be pleasant and the unpleasant ones cease to be unpleasant. What makes the pleasant states pleasant is our attachment to them, our desire to maintain them. What makes the unpleasant states unpleasant is our fear of them. Without desire or fear, the pleasantness and unpleasantness of states comes to an end. Everything becomes neutral. If that is not your experience and you think you are meditating, you are simply telling yourself a story. Ask yourself again, what is it that you are looking for, truth or a pleasant state?

Understand that likes and dislikes arise about either images in the mind such as, "he likes me" or, "he doesn't like me," or about bodily sensations that are in fact unaccepted tensions. We create the tension in the first place and we then create one more layer of tension by our non-acceptance of the initial tension.

Usually, we want a result that we can observe. We want to be present when the result occurs. We want an object. See this mechanism. If it were to happen that way, the release of this tension would just be one more object. "Enlightenment" would be simply one more object, one more expectation.

We are already light. That which is seeing these words right now is the light itself. We are already it and always have been. Let go of everything else, body, senses, and mind. Surrender everything to this light from moment to moment. Don't desire any privileged directions for the unfolding of the body, the senses, the mind, or the world. Our desire for the situation to unfold in a certain direction is part of the situation. It is this very desire that has to unfold, that has to be released.

Surrender the body, thoughts, and feelings to the consciousness in which they appear from moment to moment. Meet all feelings, sensations, and perceptions with this benevolent indifference. For a while, they will still arise, but who cares? What is truly present is your presence, invisible yet unavoidable, self-evident, ever-present.

Just stay in not knowing. Forget, from moment to moment, that which was present the moment before. Let it go. Don't hold on to anything, any method, any thought, any feeling, any bodily sensation, any sense perception. Let it flow. Make sure that there isn't a subtle expectation at the level of the body, that some sensation you don't like is going to evolve in the way you would like it to evolve.

There is a great freedom in the "I don't know." It is such a relief to give up knowing.

It is beautiful. We are innocent like a child, free from the past, free from the known, free from bondage. That which arises as a result of this unknowing is miraculous, it has a perfume. When we live in this, what we say is meaningless to anyone who takes it logically. You could say that when we know, we don't know, and that when we don't know, we know. It has meaning for those who know and for those who don't!

When we are in not knowing, we are at the threshold of the Absolute. From there, we receive everything we need at any given moment. If we need knowledge or intelligence, we receive it. The same is true if we need love or beauty. If we need nothing, we receive nothing. We are connected with the root of everything, so we are in total harmony. That is why we are struck by innocence, for example, a young animal.

೮ಽ

Sometimes I see "I am" as a function, a witnessing.

Even if we say it is a function, it is still limiting because it has a dynamic quality to it. It is also a universal rest. In the gospel according to Thomas, Jesus says to his disciples, "If they say to you, 'Where have you come from?' say to them, 'We have come from the light.' If they ask you, 'What is the sign of the light in you?' say to them, 'It is a movement and a repose.'" Not only a movement, not only a repose.

It is easy to visualize consciousness as illuminating but not so easy to see that the manifestation is itself that same consciousness.

The sage Krishna Menon uses the example of faces carved in rock. He says that at first, we only see the faces. After we have enjoyed them for a while, we lose interest, relax the focus of our attention and notice the rock in between them. When we look at the faces again, we see that they are also made out of rock. The faces represent objects; the rock in between the faces represents witnessing consciousness, and seeing the rock in the faces represents the understanding that objects are made out of consciousness.

It is a bit like a mirror, in that the objects in the mirror are nothing but glass.

Exactly. Before we realize the existence of the mirror, we are like a cat that sees another cat in the mirror and tries to catch it. When the cat bumps into the mirror, that is the equivalent of realizing the witnessing consciousness. That is Nirvikalpa samadhi, realization of the witnessing consciousness, the experience of the mirror, the subjective experience of pure consciousness. When we return to the images, they are no longer real in the sense of existing separately, outside of consciousness, made out of matter. We realize that they are nothing other than the mirror. That is Sahaja samadhi, our natural state.

The repose is the invisible presence of the mirror. The mirror is in fact at rest, but the ever-changing images that appear in it are what we call the mind. The movement also is nothing other than the mirror. We cannot say that there is just rest and no movement. Nor can we say there is only movement.

If we are the mirror, then we must be everything in the mirror. The mirror is so obvious that it is missed.

Yes, the mirror is the open secret. In the gospel according to Thomas, it says, "If you want to hide an object, put it in plain sight for everyone to see." It is the same secret that Lao Tse speaks of when he says, "The Tao that can be spoken of is not the Tao."

Does this collection of conditioning and memories, which we call the person, continue when no one is left?

It is not important whether an I-image is left, but instead whether this concept still has credibility. For instance, I was brought up with the concept that babies are born in cabbages, but having had three children, this concept has lost its credibility! It may or may not arise, but who cares?

In practice the concept and the feeling of being a separate person need to be constantly fed and reinforced. When we no longer feed this concept or this feeling, they appear less and less. However, it is dangerous to say "never." How do we know what is around the corner? It is only the ego that wants this kind of absolute perfection at the level of the body and the mind. If we are truly detached, we have no agenda with the ego, with the thought or feeling of separation, either for or against. It has no power over us. Only the ego wants to get rid of the ego.

It is a matter of detachment from the concept of being a person that is important. It is the experience of what we truly are that detaches us from this notion. It is not enough to understand the nature of the snake; we have to see the rope. It is not enough to understand that there is no snake. We have to see that which appears as the alleged snake in full light, otherwise, next time, although we may be free from one snake, it will seem as if there is another. This is the direct path. We go directly to our true nature and from there, all the confusion at the level of the mind and the body is gradually cleared up.

14

The Desire for the Absolute

I am not afraid of dying and everything is OK. Is there more than this?

If what you say is completely true, that you are not afraid of dying, there is nothing more. However, not being afraid of dying has to be understood as much more than simply not being afraid that this body might die. It implies that you have no fear that what you are, whatever that is, could possibly die. This in turn implies that you know for certain what you are. If you know what you are, that you are peace itself, there is no fear, and you no longer fuel the agitation of the mind or the restlessness of the body. Then the awareness of this peace that is inherent in what you are, starts to shine through the layer of thoughts and feelings, and they become thinner and thinner. This means that you have no attraction whatsoever for states of mind, samadhis, or ecstatic states. If they show up, of course you enjoy them, but they are figments of your imagination. It is for you to know whether this description matches the situation you describe.

It is a relief to move out of the turmoil of desire, but it seems that one is then in a void. Does one need to stay in this void for long enough to appreciate the greater reality?

There are two kinds of void, objective and subjective. Objective void is simply the absence of an object, for example, an absence of thoughts, sensations, or perceptions. It is referred to as "objective" because the absence of an object still has objective qualities. In other words, you are still looking with the same external sense organs, in the case of an absence of sensations and perceptions, or with the same mind, in the case of an absence of thoughts, that you were using during the presence of an object. You are still looking outwards in the direction of objects only to assert that there are none. That would be objective nothingness, which is an absence of characteristics. This absence still has a quality, is still a subtle object, and therefore doesn't have the real perfume.

This absence is good for the mind and the body, and you can rest in it. However, you will soon get bored with it and realize that it has no flavor, that it is not fulfilling. After a while therefore, you will start to search for a new, more fulfilling object, and this cycle of searching for objects will continue to repeat itself until you deeply understand that what you are looking for is not an object.

This understanding paves the way for the experience of what you call the greater reality, the subjective void. Subjective void is the presence in which everything appears, exists, and disappears. The existence or non-existence of any object is irrelevant with respect to this presence. This presence is empty but it is also full. It is fullness itself. It is continuous, ever-present. This presence is the perfume.

206

Is the idea to rest as this presence?

To rest as this presence doesn't make sense, because we are always this presence, whether we know it or not. However, it would make sense to rest knowingly as this presence. This implies the absence of the notion that I am not this presence, that I am something other than this presence, such as a body or a mind. When such a notion vanishes, this presence shines. It does so because it is self-luminous. It shines by itself. Then it could be said that we are knowingly this presence.

The question of resting as this presence takes on a different meaning once we have had a glimpse of it. Once we have had this glimpse, it comes back again and again. It invites us again and again. It invites us by making us aware of the ignorant thought that we are something other than this presence. Then we drop this thought and as soon as it is dropped, this presence is here again shining by itself. The presence is not absent during the ignorant thought; it just seems to be obscured by it.

We don't do anything in this presence. It has a dynamism of its own. We appear to collaborate with it, but the very desire to collaborate comes from an intuition of presence itself, from a glimpse. We don't choose this glimpse, so in fact it is only this presence collaborating with itself in order to reveal itself. There is something that is sometimes described as a deepening of this presence in time, although really that is absurd. It seems to match our experience, but it is not consistent with our understanding.

In the coming out of what we are not, there is a fraction of a second in which this presence is available.

Yes, it is very important to have the experience of it in the absence of objects, because from that moment on, we stop being afraid of it and begin to look for it instead. We love it. In the beginning, we don't have the skill to find it easily, but at some point, our search comes to an end, and it comes to an end in this presence. As we dive more and more frequently and knowingly into this presence, we understand deeply that objects arise out of it. When a fish comes out of water, it is still wet with the water in which it was immersed. Similarly, when a thought, perception, or sensation arises out of this presence, it is still saturated with it. This quality of presence seems to wear off quite rapidly but, strangely enough, it shines shortly before the object merges with presence, as the object vanishes. Therefore, at the beginning and the end of the manifestation of an object, we start to experience this light. It is like an arch that builds itself. At some point, this presence is continuous throughout the manifestation of objects although, at these times, it is more subdued than when we dive completely into it.

At the receipt of an impression, there is a point at which we give attention. Then there is only that impression arising, and it is strangely attractive. The teaching is that the mind can only have one impression at a time.

That is true, but this impression can be quite complex.

Yes, and very fast. However, in placing full attention and almost losing yourself, you experience a sort of ecstasy.

Yes, but for that approach to be successful, you have to understand that a mere concentration on the object won't suffice. In fact, it is the opposite that is required. It is a complete relaxation of the focus of our attention from the object itself, that leaves the presence aware of itself, in spite of the appearance of an object. The intensity of an object decreases as it disappears, and our experience of presence seems to become correspondingly stronger. In fact, the presence doesn't become any stronger; it is just that we are no longer distracted from it by objects.

We could compare this to something that occurs during a play. The objects are like the actors on stage. If the play is interesting and we are absorbed in the plot, we tend not to be aware of the set. At the end of the play, all the actors leave the stage and then we cannot help but notice the set. If we see the play often, it may happen that, as the play is about to finish, we relax our attention from the actors and see the set, although the actors are still present. However, once we know the play so well that we no longer have to pay attention to what the actors say or do, we see the set even during the presence of the actors, because we are no longer hypnotized by them.

ᘓ

Does mind have a choice?

Mind has no choice.

Choice makes it sound like an entity, something or someone who has a choice.

Consciousness is freedom itself, so it chooses everything at every moment. It even chooses the one who feels that he does or does not have a choice. That feeling is chosen at that moment by consciousness. That is why it is so tricky. It is very well made!

209

Why would consciousness choose to be depressed or angry or mean?

It chooses to play this game. It can write it into the play. It writes it out of its own freedom, but it can also stop it at any moment. We think everything is solid, but in fact, everything is just full of emptiness. It is like Swiss cheese. The cheese is the equivalent of this emptiness, which is the true reality of everything. What we see, touch, and think are like the holes in the cheese, the apparent gaps in the continuum of consciousness. It is this continuum of consciousness that gives form to everything that we experience. That which gives everything form is the very thing which we call "I," that which we truly are. It is this place that cannot be touched, that cannot be reached because it is so close. It is the impersonal "I."

The moment that we see ourselves as personal entities, a dilemma is created. On the one hand, we are aware of our limitations as personal entities, and therefore, there is no freedom. On the other hand, we have this intuition of our innate freedom. Therefore, in contradiction with our experienced lack of freedom, we have the intuition of free will and freedom, and this comes directly from consciousness. This conflict finds its resolution the moment we understand that we are talking about two different worlds, two different levels. At the level of the personal entity, we have no freedom at all; at the level of consciousness, we are absolute freedom. In terms of a personal entity, we cannot understand the absolute freedom that we are. We have to relinquish the notion of being a personal entity and at that moment, we find ourselves as this freedom spontaneously and naturally. Then no question arises.

Choiceless awareness means awareness that doesn't have an afterthought. It simply says, "Yes" or "No," to whatever it has just produced. What is produced is created out of its own will, so there is no second-guessing it. Choiceless awareness sees its own perfection. In the Bible it says that on the seventh day, God took a rest and saw that everything was good. There is nothing to change. Everything is created in the moment, so if choiceless awareness wants to change anything, it just changes it in the moment.

Does consciousness need to ask questions?

Consciousness is in fact playing a game with itself. Whatever is being done, consciousness is doing it. What we call "good" and what we call "evil" are equally the deed of consciousness. It is a question of whose ultimate goal consciousness is. Such a question arises out of the desire to experience consciousness. The desire to experience consciousness comes from the experience of consciousness. That is the meaning of the saying in the Bible, "You wouldn't be looking for me if you didn't already know me."

The desire for the Absolute comes from the Absolute. Although everything is the deed of consciousness, to seek consciousness knowingly is a special kind of deed. It is not an ordinary type of activity. It comes from grace. Everything is grace, but to seek grace is a special grace.

What we can understand through words on their own is simply the tip of the iceberg. With feeling and perceiving we understand the rest. We need to be in touch with the totality of our experience in order to be able to welcome it in its totality. As long as there is a lack of welcoming, somewhere we remain stuck with an object.

ೞ

Can you say something about the importance of meditation in relation to everyday life?

Remember that meditation is not an activity. Meditation is about not knowing, not wanting, not holding on to anything. We are open-handed, open-minded, open-bodied, and open-hearted.

If there is agitation of the mind, simply be the witness of it. Practical thinking can be postponed until after the meditation. Higher reasoning, thinking about the truth, can be part of the meditation. Involved psychological thinking can be used to reveal the lie upon which it is founded.

If there is psychological thinking, ask the question, "Who is this thinking about? Who is the one who is allegedly going to profit from this thinking? Who is the beneficiary?" That immediately switches the involved thinking into higher reasoning, into which it dissolves. Higher reasoning destroys the foundation of false, ignorant thinking.

Gradually, there is less and less thinkingness and more feelingness. Beautiful feelings, higher feelings, are part of the meditation. The practical feelings tell us a practical message, such as, "I'm hungry" or, "I have pain here or there." They are analogous to practical thinking. Unless there is an emergency, they can be postponed until after the meditation, and so we are left with involved feelings, negative feelings. These are the resistances, the sense of lack, the drive to do something, the boredom, the doubts, the fear, the desire, the envy. We should not indulge in these feelings but interrogate them directly at the level of feeling, tracing them back to the presence in which they arise.

This tracing back of the feeling to its source is what we call "higher feeling." If we move along a feeling upstream towards the source, it is higher feeling. If we move along a thought upstream towards the source, it is higher thinking, higher reasoning. When a feeling appears, don't stick to it. We shouldn't be afraid of our fear; neither should we do what our fear tells us to do. Rather, seek the source in which it originates, the presence. Trace the fear back to the welcoming space. The source is always bigger than the feeling that appears in it. We move away from the object into this space, into this conscious presence. In this process, there will be intermediary feelings, transformational feelings that are analogous to the intermediary thoughts that we have about the truth in higher reasoning, until they merge in presence.

Although this meditation is not an activity or a practice, it is not passive either. It is passive in the sense that there is not a personal doer doing it and no personal goal to be reached. It is active in the sense that it is not devoid of higher activity, such as higher reasoning or higher feeling. Any activity that is impersonal, which comes from the source and goes towards the source is part of the meditation. In this way, there is no clear-cut separation between meditation and daily life. There is no separation because meditation encompasses both activity and repose.

Don't worry if everything is not clear. It will eventually become clear if you are interested. Meditate from what you understand about meditation, such as benevolent indifference, or welcoming the totality of your experience without exceptions, or remaining in not knowing, or just being as you are without goals, or offering your thoughts, sense perceptions, and feeling to the presence in which they arise. Any of these suggestions will take you to meditation. The moment you have the goodwill to try them, meditation reaches its perfection. Although it may not seem to you to have reached its perfection, it reaches its perfection at the moment of goodwill. The reason you may think it is not perfect is because you construe meditation as a pleasurable state, which it is not. Meditation is not a state. It is freedom from all states.

Some of us think that a number of conditions have to be met in order to meditate. We think we must be at home, sitting on the floor with incense burning and flowers. We must be on vacation in the perfect house and the perfect orientation. All of these are simply the ego postponing the moment of its execution. Instead, we should develop an eagerness to seize the fleeting moments between two activities, such as sitting in a bus, waiting at the dentist, or taking a rest at work. Three seconds of spontaneous meditation that happen when we seize the moment have more value than hours of false meditation towards a goal, towards a personal goal. It is not a question of duration. It is a question of intensity and spontaneity. That is all it takes to take us right to the Absolute. As we become more and more one-pointed, we will develop the skill to seize these moments. And these moments will seem to become more and more frequent until they become one single moment. It is called the stabilization process.

Understand also that any activity that comes out of pure joy is not separate from meditation. It is part of it. Joy is the seal of the sacred, the seal of the divine. Psychological suffering, misery, is the seal of ignorance. It is the rejection of what we are and a futile attempt to replace it with what we are not. It is ridiculous and preposterous, the source of all good comedy.

We should make our interaction with others part of our meditation practice. In this way, we will never be out of meditation, whether we are with our co-workers, customers, employer, employees, strangers, family, friends, or simply on our own. These are wonderful opportunities to meditate, to practice higher reasoning and higher sensing, in the presence of others. In your interaction with others, practice benevolent indifference, listening to and welcoming what they say, do, or project, and also your own responses, without resistance. That will go a long way in transforming our life.

The sitting meditation we do in our bedroom once or twice a day is simply a preparation for the real meditation, to the big meditation, twenty-four hours a day, seven days a week. If we practice in the privacy of our bedrooms, it will be easier and more natural to practice during the day. However, it will still require goodwill and desire to do so during the day. If we don't do so, everything we have learned here will remain frozen. It will not die, but it will remain a frozen embryo. However, if we practice it in daily life, it will permeate our life with sweetness.

15

The Transparent Diamond

When I see that the world arises in me, there is no sense of participation, but this understanding leaves and I am involved again.

The important point about this experience is the revelation of the open secret. When this revelation happens for the first time, it is often accompanied by an exhilarating feeling of freedom and joy. This feeling is the objective aspect of the experience. The revelation of the open secret itself is the subjective aspect, the true substance of the experience. There is a tendency to forget the revelation and become attached to the objective aspect that accompanied it, to make an image of it. It is as if God reveals herself surrounded by trumpeting angels, and we tend to fall in love with the music and forget the revelation of God, which is invisible, inconceivable, and untouchable.

Having been beguiled by the objective aspect of the experience in this way, we become attached to it and then, when it disappears, we develop nostalgia for it. This nostalgia comes from the ego, together with a sense that everything would be perfect if only we could reproduce the original feeling. Forget about reproducing the feeling; what is important is to receive the revelation.

The revelation itself is timeless. It is the presence of the mirror of consciousness, that in which and as which all our experience occurs. It is the same mirror that is understanding these words right this moment. It has never vanished, unlike the experience of the angels.

It is not necessarily a pleasant feeling.

We shouldn't insist that God show up on our own terms, which are always conditioned by past experience. We want trumpets and angels, but this time God wants to appear as a warrior! We have to be open to seeing any of the possible faces of God at every moment.

I always thought that it would feel like love, but sometimes what turns up is very uncomfortable.

This feeling of discomfort has to be seen as one more reflection in the mirror. If we identify with the reflection, it means that we have not noticed the mirror, the true revelation. That which is revealed in each moment is the open secret of the presence of the now. All problems vanish when we refer directly to the revelation itself, but we forget what the true import of our experience is, where the true meaning is. We fall in love with a beautiful box, in which a transparent diamond has been placed, forgetting that the true gift is the colorless, transparent diamond. The box is so rich and full of color that we fall in love with it, but it doesn't have the same value as the diamond.

The open secret sounds so obvious.

It is this very obviousness that hides it. The mind is too complicated for the simplicity of the secret.

The mind is not content with being simple.

Yes.

So is the idea just to stay with whatever presents itself?

Yes, but also allow it to evolve freely. Staying with it doesn't mean to crystallize it. It means to be with it lovingly, in freedom, without trying to reject it, take hold of it, or even understand it. Just respect it; let it have its own life.

Is that also true of tensions that don't yield easily because they are so deeply established?

Don't try to make them yield. If they want to yield, that's fine, but if they don't want to, that's also fine. Don't make your happiness a hostage of their yielding. Don't feel that you have to have an extraordinary experience. It is our ordinary experience that is itself extraordinary. Usually, we are unable to see this. We tend to reject whatever situation arises in the moment because it doesn't quite conform to our idea of how things should be. It is not special enough. We have to see clearly that it is precisely this rejection that makes the experience seem ordinary. When we stop escaping it, it reveals its extraordinariness. Having rejected this moment, we then imagine how things should really be. We conceive the ideal experience, the true spiritual experience, which is always something other than this moment, somewhere else, and at some other time. We then start to seek this extraordinary experience, failing to notice that this cycle of dissatisfaction, rejection, and seeking recreates itself perpetually.

Just stick to the ordinary circumstances without labeling them ordinary. Be open to them with no desire to change them in any way. They are, in fact, already magical and miraculous. They are the revelation of the Absolute. The mountains, for instance, are already miracles. We don't need a little angel on top of the mountain to make it more miraculous, so don't make one up.

217

If something happens to my body, I use the mind to remind myself that it is not happening to me, that it is happening to my body.

It is very good to use the mind to readjust the way that we perceive our body. When we look at our body from this perspective, it becomes objectified, it is seen as an object of consciousness, out there in front of us. When our body is seen in this way, it is not possible to think, "I am this object out there." It is only when the body is not completely objectified, when some aspect of it is not clearly seen, that there is the possibility of thinking or feeling that it is "me."

If the body is an object and I, as consciousness, am its subject, is this not duality?

In order to free ourselves from the illusion that we are the body, we first have to become fully aware that it is an object of our attention. As we become established in this understanding, we begin to look for the boundary that separates us, consciousness, from this perceived object, and the closer we look, the more deeply we realize that it does not exist. We begin to understand that the body is an object in consciousness, not merely of consciousness. As this understanding deepens, we begin to ask ourselves what this object, which is obviously in consciousness, is actually made of, and it dawns on us that it is made of consciousness, for there is nothing else out of which it can be made. We realize the body, along with everything else, as consciousness, not simply in consciousness.

Therefore, the understanding of the body as an object of consciousness is a step that is necessary in almost all cases. However, it is not the complete understanding of our experience. There is a progression of understanding from "I am the body" to "I am nothing" to "I am everything." "I am the body" is Savikalpa samadhi. "I am nothing" is Nirvikalpa samadhi. "I am everything" is Sahaja samadhi, our natural state.

യ

218

I keep being swamped by pain.

The pain has now gone, so it was obviously not your body. You are attached to your interpretation of the origin of the pain. You think that the pain was happening inside your body, but that is just a theory. In fact, it was your actual experience that the pain was happening inside consciousness, inside you. If you let the object, the feeling of physical pain in this case, completely unfold, then there is no longer any possibility of feeling that it is you.

It was so strong that I couldn't welcome it.

Yes, there are moments when this happens, but ultimately they don't change anything. Don't let these moments of intense pain disturb the clearer and far more prevalent times when this identification is not taking place. When we are completely involved with a sensation, there is nothing we can do. Then this involvement diminishes and we realize we were unnecessarily identified.

What usually makes us feel that we are the body are tiny contractions or localizations, which in themselves are not an issue. If we simply experience them as they are, in easy situations to begin with, we get a taste of how it feels to remain uninvolved. We just experience everything the way it really is, as an appearance within consciousness. We do not have to question whether or not to become involved. We simply remain as we really are, as that within which and ultimately as which everything appears.

This is the great understanding about the inclusion of bodily sensations in our meditation. It doesn't have to go through the mind. Simply seeing the appearance as it is, an object in awareness, disidentifies us from it. When we have disentangled ourselves from the object in this way, there is no longer any personal connection with it that could subsequently trigger thoughts such as, "I am the body" or "I am pain." Just leave everything alone. You, consciousness, are fine, and the objects that appear in it are also fine. Don't tamper with anything.

219

This impartial attitude will itself have an effect on what appears within consciousness and, for no apparent reason, we will find that the conflicts in our life begin to diminish. However, that is not the goal; it is one possible outcome. There is no goal. There may still be pain but deep inside something is free from it, beyond it, behind it, and all around it. To begin with, it is not obvious, but as the background appears to be more and more present, we start to feel it in circumstances in which we would usually be completely involved, and this is the beginning of detachment.

The direct path is often misconstrued as a process involving someone who comes here, asks the right question, receives the right answer, and leaves liberated. But in reality, there is no individual entity called "I" that is coming and going. There is no one who becomes free. There is only freedom. This notion of a person who comes and goes, who asks and answers, is only a story for children. The direct path doesn't necessarily mean short; it just means direct. We go straight to the absolute truth of our experience, directly to the feeling-understanding that we stand as consciousness at every moment.

To begin with, we have an inkling of this truth. Then, the first question that we ask on encountering this perspective, if we are genuinely asking for truth, soon results in a glimpse of our true nature. Subsequently, there is one glimpse after another and something begins to change. It is like a photograph being developed. Everything comes out simultaneously in all realms of our experience: the way we understand life, the way we feel about people, animals, situations, and events, our relationships, our profession. Everything in our life is permeated by this understanding. The background comes to the foreground just as the black tones come out of the photographic paper. It is a revelation.

There is a discomfort that comes from a feeling of separation. Just witnessing this discomfort doesn't seem to be enough to dissolve it.

There is a misunderstanding. Don't just witness it. Welcome it. To welcome it means not to entertain the desire to get rid of it or change it in any way. Your question indicates that there is such a desire. We have to be prepared to live with this feeling of discomfort forever. From then on, how the feeling evolves is of no concern to us. As long as we think that the presence or the absence of the feeling makes any difference at all, then even if it does disappear, another one will soon appear. It is a bottomless bag of uncomfortable feelings. Therefore, it is important not to care. We just give up doing anything about the bag. Just welcome the presence of the bag. After all, what does it really matter if we know we are not the bag?

It is the same with the feeling of separation. We have to love it. The feeling of separation is the ego. If we try to get rid of it, we separate ourselves from it and create an ego killer, which is another face of the same thing. It's better to stick to one ego!

C３

The sun is always shining but the clouds obscure it.

The cloud is the thought that I am a person. The biggest cloud of all is the thought that I am a person who is free from the cloud. It is also a cloud to think that I am a person who is bound by the cloud.

We are here for one single purpose, which is to experience love. Love is the experience that consciousness, that which we are, is not personal. In order to experience love, we have to be open to it. We have to be open to the possibility that what we truly are, consciousness, that which is seeing and understanding these words right this moment, is not personal. We are all it. The bodies and minds that appear in it are all different, but that in which they appear, that which sees and experiences, is always one and the same. It knows itself as consciousness in each one of us, as each one of us. When we are open to it, it resonates. When we catch this resonance in the heart, it radiates as love. When we catch it in the mind, it appears as understanding. When it is revealed in the world, it shines as beauty. They are all the same thing, consciousness revealing itself to itself in different ways. This is how it knows itself, by resonating in this way. It is like when somebody says, "You!" something in us responds, resonates. Before we are a mind or a body, we are this "I am."

In our meetings we turn our attention away from objects, towards the source. We are constantly being reminded of the source. We might wonder how it is possible to turn our attention towards something that is invisible, inconceivable, and incomprehensible. However, each time we withdraw the focus of our attention from objects, we are in fact turning towards the source and, each time we do this, we vanish as a person.

Every time we are reminded of this unknown direction, we look towards the source and we vanish into it, we are taken by it. Then the mind arises again, the old habit of focusing exclusively on objects, and we seem to forget, until the nostalgia returns and we are taken again. When this happens often enough, life begins to change for us. The way we perceive, see, and understand, changes. Our actual experience changes. To begin with, we feel a causeless joy filtering in between the objects, through the gaps. Then it begins to permeate the objects themselves, our thoughts, our body, the world. The things that we always thought of as being solid begin to feel transparent and that which we thought was fleeting and ephemeral, consciousness, becomes more tangible and stable. This is the open secret of satsang.

The only thing that we need to remember is, "I don't know." Nobody knows. I am here sitting in a chair like someone who knows, but I don't know. It just happens, I don't know how. Every time it happens, I am amazed.

This afternoon, I thought that I didn't know that which is unknowable, and then I realized that this can't be true, it's just words.

For people who don't understand, that has no meaning, but for those who do, it has all the meaning in the world. Parmenides said, "Being is and non-being is not." To the philosopher interested in logical statements, it is a tautology. A good satsang is one of which you remember nothing. In fact, nothing is said. Satsang is silence. Nothing remains, but you feel good. Its essence is lightness, love, or beauty. That is all. It cannot be spoken of.

It seems that the only thing we can do is polish the mirror. Is this done by not knowing?

Instead of trying to maintain an attitude of not knowing, it would be simpler to understand that we cannot know anything. Then we don't have to maintain any attitude. That is a fact of life. We don't know that which knows everything. So how, therefore, can we truly know any of the things that it is supposed to know? We cannot. So we know nothing.

We are that which knows but which is itself unknowable. To know that which knows is not knowledge of an object. Our true identity is that which we are. It could be said that the unknowing of objects is a prerequisite for the knowing of our true nature.

There is a story of the fifth patriarch of Zen, who said that he would transmit the bowl and the robe, the sign of office of patriarch, to whoever could write the best poem about the truth. He had a very good disciple who wrote a poem on the wall, and nobody dared write another after him because he was obviously the best. In his poem he said that the soul is like a mirror and we should keep polishing it to make sure that not the slightest speck of dust damages the surface. The patriarch approved it and said it was a nice poem that reflected the deep meaning of Zen.

There was another monk working in the kitchen who wrote an answer saying that the essence of the Self is pure, so there was no danger of any speck of dust staining it. This mirror, he said, was of a different nature than the dust, so why bother cleaning it? When the patriarch saw this reply, he knew that it was the real thing, the direct path. That is how the sixth patriarch of Zen came to be. So no polishing, but if you want to polish, that's fine!

It seems that the job of the mind is to know and yet it cannot.

All the mind has to do is to get out of the way. The mind gets out of the way when we understand that it cannot secure happiness, no matter what it does. We have to see clearly that the happiness that follows the acquisition of a desired object is derived from the fact that, for a brief moment, we are desireless and therefore happy. When we understand that our happiness comes from this desirelessness and not from objects, the mind naturally comes to a rest.

Once it has been fully understood that the mind cannot be the architect of its own happiness, why does it continue to produce desires for objects?

The problem is with the dissatisfaction that prompts us to look for happiness in objective experience in the first place and which keeps returning, again and again, in spite of the happiness we experience on fulfillment of a desire. We have to see that this process will continue as long as we neglect our feelings and bodily sensations and concentrate our inquiry and meditation in the mind only. When feelings become too intense or unpleasant, we usually generate thoughts as a distraction from the unpleasantness, and we escape into thinking.

The mind in this way acts as a sort of screen, producing desires and their subsequent activity in order to avoid these uncomfortable feelings. However, they are unpleasant only as long as we don't face them. The moment we face them they become harmless. When they are neutralized in this way, there is no longer any need for us to generate thoughts in order to distract ourselves from them. Therefore, both the mind and the body have to be free of the tensions that create this dissatisfaction and its subsequent train of desires and, in that moment, we have the opportunity of seeing that we are already happiness itself.

224

Thoughts manifest through language and enable us to conceptualize, and these concepts in turn either lead to freedom or depression.

Thoughts are usually preceded by an image before being formulated in words. The thought itself is a formulation of this image. However, there are also thoughts that arise out of thin air. These are inspired thoughts, like poetic insight, which come in a flash, and we subsequently find the words to fit the thought. There are other thoughts that come from the past, from memory, from recurrent thinking, whose origin is the I-thought. That is captive thinking, dependent on the past. The thinking that is fresh and comes in the now is free thinking. Captive thinking binds us. Free thinking liberates us.

We don't have to remember in order simply to be, and yet there is a flavor of remembering in this being. Is this some higher memory?

We could call it remembrance. The difference between memory and remembrance is that memory refers to objects, whereas remembrance refers to the subject. Memory refers to the past, whereas remembrance refers to the timeless. When we are free from the past, there is inspiration. We fall from grace when we bring in the ego. It is like a balance artist dancing on a cable, perfectly at ease until he remembers the abyss.

If one could stay in "not knowing" without reaching out for the next branch to cling to, there would be complete insecurity, which at the same time is security.

Yes. That is what satsang is about. It is not about exchanging concepts but about dancing on the cable. Once we are on the cable there is no disciple or teacher; there is only dancing. All the watching bystanders are also dancing with us. Satsang is an art form: how to dance spontaneously with inspiration.

It is a relief not to have to live up to external expectations. With that comes spontaneity and humor.

Sometimes humor and at other times something else. Sometimes it is sweetness or relaxation. It doesn't have to be one way or the other. It can change dramatically from one moment to the next.

Something that prevents spontaneous questioning in satsang is the ego saying, "I already know the answer."

That is not necessarily the ego because it might well be true. The way to find out is to ask yourself whether your own answer puts an end to your question. If it does, it was the right answer. It is good to be autonomous and get the answer that way. In fact, when you receive the answer in this way, it comes from exactly the same place as an answer that comes from the teacher. Truth is not the possession of the teacher, so whether the answer comes to you directly or whether it comes via the so-called teacher, it always comes from the same place, from consciousness.

CB

I find that I try to get away from the quietness in meditation. I get bored and don't know how to welcome it. There is no juice there.

Be interested in your boredom. There is no juice because you are expecting something and you are not interested in understanding. You want juice but you do not want to learn where the grapes are and how to press them. We understand boredom by being interested in boredom. We cannot understand something in which we have no interest and from which we are trying to escape. See how boredom triggers thoughts. If we want the mind to be quiet and undisturbed, we first have to face boredom. If we stop facing the feeling of boredom, we escape from it into thinking, and this subsequent mental agitation then triggers all sorts of activities with which we become involved.

When we face the boredom, no matter how unpleasant it is, without labeling or judging, the mind and the body become quiet and, as a result, we do not get involved in useless activities. Then we can see it for what it is, a cluster of bodily sensations, an aversion. It is very deeply rooted in us and is not going to dissolve in one minute. However, every time we welcome it, the boredom loses something of its unpleasantness. We find ourselves identifying with it less and less and, as we do so, it begins to lose its capacity to distract us from the source. It becomes clear that this very boredom has been one of the main motivating forces in our life.

Is it boredom that compels me to seek the truth?

Boredom is an invitation from God. It is a great opportunity. If we want to get rid of boredom, we are declining the invitation and trying to replace it with an offer of our own making. Boredom comes from the feeling that whatever is current, whatever is or is not happening at this moment is not interesting, and so we look for a distraction, for entertainment.

I know that there is no real juice in objects, but there is still the desire for juice.

Yes, but you are still subtly looking for a happy state. As long as you are looking for a happy state and not for truth, there will be a conflict. See clearly the mechanisms of escaping from the present moment and how we project the possibility of happiness into some future situation. We should go right to the source of this boredom. The boredom is not an end in itself. It is a feeling, an aversion, an imaginary wall felt in the body. It is made of localizations in the body. It is no big deal. It is just a localization. It is not painful, merely unpleasant. You want to get away from it, which means that you are not yet welcoming it.

My suggestion is to fully welcome it until it is no longer a concern, until it is neutral, just a sensation. Make a deep acquaintance with it. This will take more than just one minute and will perhaps lead elsewhere, to other, subtler feelings. However, the moment we have the slightest intention to get rid of it by welcoming it, we are no longer welcoming it. Welcoming is not simply welcoming the boredom, it is welcoming the totality of the situation. Boredom is only one tree in the landscape. Don't focus on it; be open to everything else. At some point the boredom will recede into the background and something else will come to the foreground. On the other hand, the desire to get rid of boredom actually maintains it in the foreground as a problem and the more we focus on a problem, the more we perpetuate it.

Boredom is an object and like all objects, it comes and goes. Welcome the totality of the situation. Give your boredom room to expand, to unfold, but without any volition in relationship to it. Be open to the totality of the situation of which boredom is only a part.

Somewhere in you, there is a refusal of the present moment, an expectation that something different should be happening. See that what we truly want to happen is in fact happening all the time, but we expect happiness to be delivered via an object. We expect this happiness on a silver plate. It is not going to work; it has never worked through an object. We have to surrender the belief that happiness is dependent on or conditioned by objects.

It seems that we have to accept this emptiness and nothingness.

It is not emptiness. You are just creating this feeling. It is your own creation. It is your own violence. In fact, there is no emptiness in the situation. It is just perfect the way it is. There is nothing wrong in the situation. Right this moment, what is wrong? If there is no juice, it means that you are not welcoming the totality of the situation; you are still doing something with a purpose. For example, if you meditate with a purpose, you might as well forget it. That is not meditation. It is end-gaining, striving. Just be simple.

You don't have to stay with your boredom once you have welcomed it completely. If you see that the situation truly has no juice, then allow it to move on. Be completely open. Do not focus on a dark state. Don't escape boredom, but don't focus on it either.

Don't maintain it. If you find that you are expecting it to leave, just face it, look at it from two or three angles. Then, if it has nothing to teach you, let it go and let the situation move on to something else.

Know that your happiness is not in the next situation, in the next object, but that the next situation or object is simply a celebration of this happiness that we already are. Stick to happiness throughout all situations. Don't stick to the situations.

We all know happiness. Follow it as it flows. The object is not the happiness, so we have to be ready to flow from moment to moment. It is only when the object vanishes that we experience happiness. The so-called happiness-bearing object delivers only when it vanishes. When it vanishes, we find ourselves as this happiness itself, as peace and bliss. If we follow our bliss from situation to situation, we will see that we stick to ourselves. Bliss is what we all know as happiness.

When I attempt to welcome feelings, they seem to increase and welcoming becomes impossible.

We should understand that welcoming doesn't apply to a specific object or feeling. We welcome the totality of the situation, whatever the situation is. If we only welcome an object, we prevent this object from evolving or from leaving, because we become attached to a given shape or flavor. If we welcome the totality of the situation, the objects themselves can undergo all kinds of transformation. We should be present to the totality of whatever arises in consciousness, instead of focusing on something that we want to get rid of. Then, we will become aware of the feeling of unhappiness, and the dislike of the feeling, and perhaps a bird singing in the distance and all kinds of things. Let all that evolve by itself. Don't try to put your hands on it. If you focus on one single thing, you are still trying to manipulate it.

There is the story of a sadhu who heard that everything was God. As he was walking down the street, a mad elephant came charging towards him. The mahout on top of the elephant cried, "Get out of the way!" The sadhu thought that as both he and the elephant were God, he would not be harmed. He ended up in hospital and when he complained to his guru, he was reminded that the mahout was also God and that God had told him to get out of the way! The sadhu had been focusing on the elephant instead of on the totality of the situation.

It seems difficult in some situations.

We focus on an object because we think that we can do something about the situation. The moment we understand that there is nothing that we, as a person, can do about any situation because we are not a doer, we let the situation evolve by itself. It is a kind of off-hand approach to the situation, a stepping back.

If we focus on an object in any situation, our natural tendency is to focus on the problematic aspect, which means to focus on our misery. This only makes us more miserable, it maintains the misery. We don't know what the totality is. We don't know how it is going to evolve. Therefore, we become interested in the situation, but without an agenda.

Do we have control over our focus of attention?

As a person, no. If we deeply understand this and remember it in any given moment, when we catch ourselves red-handed trying to manipulate a situation, we can immediately let go of the desire to manipulate. Then something happens. The situation becomes free to evolve in an organic way.

We should have a basic interest in life, a feeling that life is good, that life is perfection. That is all that is needed: trust. Trust in the divine. "Be still and know that I am God." Just be quiet, don't worry, and see what happens. Give God a chance.

Could you speak of my will and thy will? How do I make a decision?

"My will" creates the mess. "Thy will" cleans it up. When you have a decision to make, it is good to try to make it from that place of stillness. Come to stillness and wait for an answer that feels good. That is all there is. It is your goodwill that matters. It is not making the right decision that matters. A good decision is one that flows out of this goodwill, which is trying to let the infinite decide. Then, it is going to be magical. Even if your decision is apparently a mistake, some miracle will intervene to fix the mistake and go beyond any expectations. Whereas if the decision comes from the person and is apparently correct, whatever has been won will be lost. It is all a game.

The preoccupation with winning or losing does not seem to be a game. When does the lightness come in?

When you are open to the idea that it is a game.

How can we keep these days of treasure together in our hearts and retain or recall the perfume of this experience knowingly?

One should forget. Don't try to recall or retain. In this way, everything that can be forgotten is forgotten, and what remains is the perfume that can never be forgotten. Don't worry. The perfume will never forget you.

All things are knowingly or unknowingly longing for the source from which they emanate, are longing for the experience of awareness. That is how the entire cosmos is set in motion, through this longing. It is the longing of the earth for the sun that makes it rotate around the sun. See the beauty of your longing, because the sun is already in the longing for the sun.

Just tune into this silence, into this presence which is you, which is us. Surrender everything that is perceived, especially your body. Leave it there, floating in emptiness, floating in your infinity, desiring nothing, having nothing, knowing nothing, being nothing.

Take a bath in this light. Turn your heart towards this resonance. Don't ask how, just do it. Do it again and again. Every time it seems you have lost it just do it again, until it becomes as natural as a young child looking back to see if his mother is still present watching him. This is a very simple gesture, going back to that which you love the most. From this place there is truly nothing to do.

Simply remain in waiting without waiting. You are the love in everything you love. You are the beauty in everything you behold. You are the intelligence in everything you understand. You are the sweetness in all things.

Just seek yourself as this sweetness. Stay focused on the sweetness and don't be attached to things. Things are the shell. The sweetness is the pearl.

Objects are like the shadow of the branches of a tree moved by the wind and projected against a wall. The kitten desperately tries to catch the shadow. Be a wise, old cat.

You do not have to eliminate the objects that appear, the sensations, the thoughts, or the feelings. Simply be indifferent to them. And if you are not indifferent to them, ask yourself, "What are these shadows going to bring about? Why do I desire them? Why am I afraid of them? Are they truly what I want?"

You know that you are, beyond a shadow of a doubt, but you don't know what you are. The mind will be forever frustrated by the question, "What am I?" The mind only knows what you are not. What you are is a mystery to the mind. It is a beautiful mystery. It cannot be uttered because it cannot be thought of.

You are the wall, the sun, the tree, the wind, and the cat.

Live with your desire for truth. Let it be your guide. The desire for truth comes from truth itself. It brings about higher intelligence that will, in time, clarify all questions.

Enjoy the path. There is already a joyful element in understanding. Don't take yourself for a limited entity, now that you have understood, at least in a glimpse, that you are awareness beyond all thoughts, feelings, and perceptions. Keep it as your treasure. Go back to it whenever it invites you. Live with this understanding and let the understanding do the work.

For information about Retreats and Dialogues with Francis Lucille, and for details of videos, books, and cassettes, please see his Web site, www.francislucille.com.